Beautiful Blessings from God

Beautiful Blessings
FROM GOD

Patricia Raybon

TYNDALE®
MOMENTUM

An Imprint of
Tyndale House Publishers, Inc.

Visit Tyndale online at www.tyndale.com.

Visit Tyndale Momentum online at www.tyndalemomentum.com.

Tyndale Momentum, the Tyndale Momentum logo, and *LeatherLike* are registered trademarks of Tyndale House Publishers, Inc. Tyndale Momentum is an imprint of Tyndale House Publishers, Inc.

Beautiful Blessings from God

Adapted from *The One Year God's Great Blessings Devotional* (2011) under ISBN 978-1-4143-3871-2 by Tyndale House Publishers, Inc.

Designed by Nicole Grimes

Published in association with the literary agency of Ann Spangler and Company, 1420 Pontiac Road SE, Grand Rapids, MI 49506.

ISBN 978-1-4964-1311-6 (LeatherLike)

Printed in India

22	21	20	19	18	17	16
7	6	5	4	3	2	1

Introduction

❦

I didn't know I was blessed. Never even imagined it.
Never dared to guess it. Not all the time, anyway.

Then one evening, while sharing a dinner with
friends, I looked at their photos from a trip to Ghana.
A smart three-year-old child—taking a soapy bath
in a bucket outdoors in a nice rain—looked in the
camera's eye and grinned. On her face? A confident
look of blessed joy.

Her humble village had only one deep well.
So when the skies suddenly opened and poured
down rain, everybody grabbed buckets to catch the
water. Then the little girl's mother handed her soap
and a towel, and the child tore off her clothes and
scrambled into a bucket. Soon she was soapy from
head to toe. And laughing about it all.

The child had a job to do in a big storm, but she
obeyed and worked through the inconvenience, the
downpour—not to mention the lack of plumbing—
and she found joy. Showered with blessings.

That's what I was seeking when I started this

devotional: to be showered with God's beautiful blessings—but not as the world thinks, in material ways. I longed to be showered with God's highest, simplest, and greatest blessings, then get refreshed on the journey—even in a storm.

A simple but brave request? In fact, the path I sought was waiting on my bookshelf, ready for me to launch ahead. So I pulled down my Bible to read. My plan? I would launch a deliberate, purposeful journey through the fresh wind of God's Word, turning to the sweet truth of God's great wisdom to uncover His beautiful and quiet blessings.

But God wasn't so quiet. Instead, He wrote in loud words. With exclamation points.

Use common sense!

Be content!

I knew I'd heard such timely advice before, but for some reason on this trip through the Bible, I saw and heard such urgings in a different way.

God seemed to be personally teaching His own rules for beautiful blessings—timeless, smart, life-giving principles of both promise and joy.

I started making notes:

"Gentleness makes us great" (see Psalm 18:35).

"God answers prayers when we trust Him" (see 1 Chronicles 5:20).

As I continued reading, I discovered that with each command to seek His high and beautiful road, God promised a simple but powerful blessing. Not just an ordinary blessing. Instead, to those who followed His virtuous path, God promised His most grandiose, extravagant, crazy, highest, greatest blessings.

This devotional is based on the premise that the secret to every desire of the Christian life—and to every desire of God to bless us—can be found by pursuing His beautiful path of virtue.

What's the best way to find it, using this devotional? Take the journey to blessings one day at a time. Go slow, letting God inspire each day's intimate searching and seeking.

As you read, I hope you will stand under God's downpour and enjoy His mighty rain. Rest in the One who promises to bless your efforts with His presence—and His power—leading you on His passage to a mighty end.

No eye has seen, no ear has heard,
no mind has conceived what God has
prepared for those who love him.

1 CORINTHIANS 2:8-9, NIV

Listening to His Voice

Listen, my child. . . .
PROVERBS 1:8

It's dark, cold, and early. But I'm excited. On this morning, the most important thing I have to do is hear from God. And not just a little bit. I want to hear without limits. Isn't that what we're all saying today? That we want to be blessed by God? So we can bless God without limits?

So I sit, like you, Bible in hand—the first chapter of Proverbs staring up at me—looking for some life-changing secret on how to make such blessings happen.

Instead, Proverbs offers a gracious and quiet word: *Listen.*

It's not a suggestion. It's a plea. Spoken tenderly. Even kindly. "Listen, my child. . . ." The writer, King Solomon, seems to know most of us *don't* listen well. We wake up talking, our voices rattling around in our heads, hollering first and hearing second.

But Solomon says *stop.*

Step off the loud, rusty, ragged treadmills of our

lives. Today, he says, turn from our noise—all the emotional chatter raging in our minds or spewing from other people. And turn it off.

Listening is serious business, to be sure. Listening to God's Word, implanted by God's Spirit in our hearts, "has the power to save your souls," says James 1:21. Why? "My sheep listen to my voice," Jesus answers. "I know them, and they follow me." When we listen, "I give them eternal life," Jesus promises, "and they will never perish. No one can snatch them away from me" (John 10:27-28). When we listen to God, He knows us. As we silence ourselves, our prayers don't perish. God may hear us better, plus, He grants us eternal life. I'm ready to try that. Quiet my heart. *And* my mouth. Then look what I'll discover: God is speaking.

A good listener is not only popular everywhere,
but after a while he knows something.
WILSON MIZNER

Listening for His Spirit

All the people listened closely.
NEHEMIAH 8:3

Curious business, this godly listening. As I try it, I hear all manner of mysteries. Great advice. Honest truth. Deep desires. So I'm hearing less gossip. Less complaining. Less doubt, fear, worry, and false teaching. I see, in fact, why our enemy overwhelms our ears with noise.

If we listen to ungodly things, we miss one of God's most beautiful blessings: hearing God's Spirit. So I quiet myself to better hear my Bible, feeling that listening seems too pretty a virtue to unlock God's mighty, delivering, trustworthy, Spirit-filled power. Then I see:

Those who refuse to listen to God prefer to go their own way—to trust in themselves. To be their own god. So God asks something simple—*just listen to Me*—knowing that those who listen truly want to know what His Spirit says.

Yet how do we hear Him?

By listening closely. That's what Jesus teaches.

Draw near, Christ says. Why? He doesn't shout. To hear Him, we sit close, see Him better, and then we learn. "The closer you listen, the more understanding you will be given—and you will receive even more" (Mark 4:24).

Theologian Richard Foster, in his book *Prayer: Finding the Heart's True Home*, describes this close approach to listening to God. "I wait quietly," he says. Tuning his heart to God's voice, he waits as "people and situations spontaneously rise" to his awareness. Letting the Spirit guide his prayer, he then remains quiet for a while, "inviting the Spirit to pray through [him] 'with sighs too deep for words.'" Throughout the day, he jots down brief prayer notes in a small journal.

Dare we do the same? Listen closely enough to hear the Spirit-filled thunder of God's clear voice? Even take notes? I dare you to try it today. Then, in your quiet, God speaks.

If the key is prayer, the door is Jesus Christ.
RICHARD FOSTER

3

Loving as God Loves

And now I will show you the most excellent way.
1 CORINTHIANS 12:31, NIV

It was a high-profile city. Worldly, too. So maybe Corinth was like the place where you live. Or the place you'd like to live. (Or the place you think you'd like to live.)

But Corinth, as "happening" as it was—this crossroads of commerce and culture—was also at the center of corruption. A moral cesspool, some called it. The Greeks even had a name—*korinthiazomai*, "to act like a Corinthian." What did it mean? To be sexually immoral. Yes, Corinth was that kind of place.

The church there, in fact, was embedded, tainted, and torn with the spirit of the city. So a sexual scandal was brewing at the church. Spiritual pride thrived there too. With church members from across the globe, all speaking various languages, the Corinthian congregation especially prided "speaking in tongues." It was talking like angels, they said.

But the apostle Paul knew better. So he wrote them a letter. Saying this:

Even if you speak like angels—speaking in tongues—if you don't love like Christ, it counts for nothing. Such fancy talk in God's ears is like a noisy gong or a clanging cymbal.

This surely got their attention. Does it get yours today?

Love is better than talk, in other words.

More than any other spiritual gift, and there are many, love is better. Better than knowledge, tithing, even prophecy. Paul wrote in detail about these gifts and others throughout the book of 1 Corinthians. But in the thirteenth chapter, known sometimes as the love chapter of the Bible, Paul makes a case for love. "The most excellent way."

Why excellent?

Because God *is* love. So love never fails. There's no better way to say it. In any language, love never fails. So bless God today by loving. Then don't forget: Let God bless you by loving you back.

Love first!
KENT HUGHES

Loving with All Knowledge

But the man who loves God is known by God.
1 CORINTHIANS 8:3, NIV

"Remember me?" A visitor at our church is shaking my hand. Big smile. Hearty handshake. I'm smiling back. In my mind, however, I'm lost and embarrassed. Her face is familiar. But in truth, I can't remember how I know her. So we talk awhile. My husband walks up. Greets her too. Knowing him, I can tell he's struggling to put a name with her face. Finally, in the car, it comes to me. "I know her," I tell him, explaining. "She rode our commuter bus." We both smile. Mystery solved.

Or was it? Because I've seen the same quizzical look on others' faces when they can't remember my name or face. I am amazed and humbled, therefore, to love a God who knows me completely—who promises that the very hairs on my head are *all* numbered (Matthew 10:30).

It's such a contrast to human knowledge. The famed nineteenth-century Baptist preacher Charles Spurgeon takes aim at human knowledge this way:

"Many men know a great deal, and are all the greater fools for it." He adds: "There is no fool so great a fool as a knowing fool." In fact, the apostle Paul warns about it: If I "knew everything about everything, but didn't love others, what good would I be?" (1 Corinthians 13:2).

So I stop congratulating myself that, finally, I know who the church visitor is. I remember her. But I don't *know* her. Not as God knows her, and not as God knows me.

How can I bless others by knowing them today? I start by loving God as He pleads. *With all your heart, all your soul, all your mind, and all your strength* (Mark 12:30). When I love God that much, I know Him more. Then He blesses me with His power so I may love and know others like He does.

There is nothing sweeter in this sad world than the sound of someone you love calling your name.
KATE DICAMILLO

The Gift of Compassion

"Right!" Jesus told him. "Do this and you will live!"
LUKE 10:28

My good friend Denise can cry a good river. Openly. Deeply. Sincerely. In a heartbeat, if she sees anybody or anything hurting—man, animal, or child—her eyes well up, and in an instant, she's reaching out to comfort, wiping away tears—and not just her own. When it comes to compassion—meaning "to suffer with"—she could write the book, and she admits it. "I *know* I feel deeply," she says.

But why don't we all feel such compassion? As in the parable of the Good Samaritan, why are more of us like the indifferent priest and the uncaring Levite—walking past, if not running past, the hurt we see and not stopping to help?

Jesus understood the problem. When an expert in religious law asked how he could obtain eternal life, the Lord offered a subtle question: "What does the law of Moses say?" The scholarly man shot back an answer: "Love God and love your neighbor as yourself," much as any churchgoer would say. We know such love is right, and Jesus agreed. "Right!" But the clever man couldn't let well enough alone. "And who is my neighbor?" Of course, Jesus replied with the parable—a story so familiar that most of us could repeat it from memory. Like the scholarly man, we know this story and its classic theme: compassion.

But Jesus reminded us of something far greater.

This parable is about eternal life. *That* is the blessing and reward for showing compassion, a deeper life in God. That life factor, indeed, prompted the clever man's question. *What must I do to inherit eternal life?* Do compassion, Jesus replied in His parable. Do *this* and you will live. Put others before self, that is—and live. It's neighborly to help. But even better, compassion allows God to bless us with His life. What a gift for sharing what God has already freely given. His compassionate help and power.

We help, because we were helped.
ANNE LAMOTT

Kindness: To Be Kept by God

*Continue in his kindness. Otherwise,
you also will be cut off.*

ROMANS 11:22, NIV

It's easy to gloat. Too easy. No surprise, then, that
gloating Gentiles arose in the early church at
Rome. These new Christians realized their special
status. They were "grafted into" God's family tree
while unbelieving Israelites were "cut off."

Yet the apostle Paul hands these Gentiles a
strong warning: "Consider therefore the kindness
and sternness of God: sternness to those who fell,
but kindness to you, provided that you continue in
his kindness. Otherwise, you also will be cut off"
(v. 22, NIV).

Sharp warning. The reminder, however, sheds
light most on God and on the nature of *His* kindness. We're not asked to emulate human kindness,
not with all of its many shortcomings. Rather the
apostle sets a higher benchmark: Continue to be
kind as God is kind.

But how is God kind? And when?

He grants us grace, even when we don't deserve it. Paul, in this story, reminds the Gentiles of exactly that by making a critical point: that, yes, the unbelieving Israelites were broken off from the family tree. But he adds: "If they do not persist in unbelief, they will be grafted in, for God is able to graft them in again" (v. 23, NIV).

He then uses a provocative image to point out that if God was willing to cut us out of a wild olive tree and graft us into a "cultivated" olive tree, "how much more readily will these, the natural branches, be grafted into their own olive tree!" (v. 24, NIV).

So we shouldn't be conceited about God's adoption of us, Paul warns. Instead, we are to be kind as God is kind—to continue in His kindness, even when others don't deserve such grace. When we continue in this way, we can be assured of a marvelous blessing: We'll never be cut off from the graciousness, goodness, and power of our God.

Kind words also produce their own image on men's souls; and a beautiful image it is.
Blaise Pascal

Generosity with Courage

One man gives freely, yet gains even more.
PROVERBS 11:24, NIV

Money was on my mind when I sat down to try to reflect on generosity. But immediately I knew I was off track. To be sure, money is one component of generosity, but hardly the first or most important. Why? For one thing, God owns everything (Psalm 50:10).

The least of what He owns, however, is money. As well, God's greatest generosity is about the gift of His Son. A priceless gift, for certain.

But what about the rest of us? To be generous, what kind of people must we be? Good-hearted and loving? Or bighearted and kind? Such traits are key. But topping my list, when it comes to generosity, is Spirit-empowered courage. A lack of fear, yes, but also trust in the all-sufficiency of God allows otherwise tightfisted people to let go and give back. When we fearlessly trust God to provide all of our needs, we demonstrate that, in giving, we are confident we won't be left not having enough.

Giving without fear. Are you giving like that?

Or are you stingy—believing that, in giving, you'll be left holding a half-empty bag? I'm aware of such people because I've been one myself. Over the years, when I was asked by pastors to tithe or by family members to lend, my first reaction was to question the request. In the end, I might give but always reluctantly. Or with limits. Or not at all.

As my prayer life keeps turning, however, and I focus not on getting things—but on getting changed—I'm surprised to discover that by seeking in prayer to know God, I end up empowered to trust God. And with trusting God comes the courage to trust Him enough to give *and let go*. Should we give wisely? Of course. Should we give prudently? Absolutely. But to give fearlessly—understanding that in giving we gain—is the most beautiful and blessed giving of all.

No one has ever become poor by giving.
ANNE FRANK

Generosity: For the Good

*The generous will prosper; those who refresh
others will themselves be refreshed.*

PROVERBS 11:25

What the world needs now is a bounty of . . .
refreshment?

In a weary world filled with poverty, crime,
despair, and all manner of evil and sin, why would
the psalmist promote refreshment? I ponder this
irony: The Bible's teachings on generosity often focus
less on the tangible than on blessings intangible.

Like refreshment.

Like the phone call I received yesterday from a
church friend. She'd missed me at the Sunday service
because I stayed home with a head cold. Her call, late
on Sunday afternoon, to say kind things—*I missed
you, I'm praying for you*—lifted my spirits and, in fact,
refreshed my soul. The next day, I felt measurably
better. Refreshed, indeed.

Did it cost her anything to pick up the phone
and call? It took time. But as we chatted, she shared
a concern about one of her adult children—and

I offered the answer she seemed to need. "Thank you!" she said as our chat drew to a close. "That's just what I needed to hear!" That is, she'd called me to offer her generous concern, but by the end of our chat, she was refreshed in return.

Theologian John Calvin explained the ironies of generosity this way: "There cannot be a surer rule, nor a stronger exhortation to the observance of it, than when we are taught that all the endowments which we possess are divine deposits entrusted to us for the very purpose of being distributed for the good of our neighbor."

Jesus said this: "Give as freely as you have received!" (Matthew 10:8).

Can we give all the time? Or give all we have?

Of course not. Yet we each can give more—more consistently and with a greater appreciation for Him who gave His all. When I give that way, somebody else will get blessed with refreshment. But often the first somebody is me.

For it is in giving that we receive.
SAINT FRANCIS OF ASSISI

9

Peace with God

Submit to God, and you will have peace.

JOB 22:21

First she lost her house. Then she lost her job. Then a long-standing health problem flared up, leaving my friend's body weary, her bank account empty, and her spirits broken. In this storm she dared ask God an angry question: "Why *me*, Lord?" Her tears fell hard. "I mean, why *me*? And how much more am I supposed to take!" Her questions, she realized later, echoed those asked by Job when the "blameless" Old Testament man lost everything—his sons and daughters, his livestock, and his good health. In painful skin sores, head to toe, he pleaded to God: "What have I done to you?" Or as he put it: "Why have you made me your target?" (Job 7:20, NIV).

With that, Job cried his way through a tortured discourse on the nature of God and the futility of man: "How can a mortal be righteous before God? . . . Who has resisted him and come out unscathed?" (Job 9:2, 4, NIV). Or as he added: "Who can say

18

to him, 'What are you doing?' . . . How then can I dispute with him? How can I find words to argue with him?" (Job 9:12, 14, TNIV). The book of Job is, indeed, a classic exploration of the questions that mere mortals dare to ask an unquestionable God. The journey, however, leads to a vital conclusion:

That despite God's love for us, God is still God. God alone. Or as the Lord said to Job: "Who has a claim against me that I must pay?" (Job 41:11, NIV). To be sure, God isn't some arbitrary, capricious dictator. Job finally repented for daring to suggest it. Instead, as he heeded the advice of his friend—to stop quarreling with God and be at peace with Him— things went well for Job.

With a renewed heart, Job even prayed for his friends. Then "the Lord restored his fortunes," giving him "twice as much as before!" (Job 42:10). My friend, as well, stopped asking, Why me? Making peace with God, she started praising Him again—not for fixing her problems, but for blessing her with the power of His Son—our peaceful Solution.

Any hurt is worth it that puts us on the path of peace.
Eugene Peterson

Peace of Mind

But the LORD said to him, "Peace! Do not be afraid."
JUDGES 6:23, NIV

M ighty warriors aren't wimps. We're not supposed to be, anyway. But in this story,
the doubting wheat farmer Gideon is skittish,
frightened, and nervous. First, the local bad guys,
the Midianites, are running roughshod over his
people—camping on their land, ruining their crops,
racing their camels over hearth and hill and home,
and scaring Gideon half out of his wits.

In the midst of it all, an angel of the Lord
appears to Gideon and addresses him as "mighty
warrior" (v. 12, NIV).

Is Gideon honored? No. He answers with doubts.
"But sir," as he puts it, "if the LORD is with us,
why has all this happened to us? Where are all his
wonders?" (v. 13, NIV).

The complaints are another way for Gideon to say
what he truly means: *I'm a wimp—and I'm afraid.* A
mighty warrior? *No way.* Or in Gideon's case, he keeps
begging for proof, finally crying, "I'm doomed!"

Fear sounds like that, and it's at the heart, for sure, of much of our worry.

So God Himself finally cuts Gideon off with one word:

Peace.

When we heed this order—choosing peace despite feeling everything but peaceful—God responds by calming our situation. Notice the order here. God doesn't step in to calm us before our problems turn to peace. In reverse order, we first invite in God's peace. *Then* God steps in, calming our fears—easing our troubled minds.

We see that same lesson in the New Testament when the apostle Paul tells the church at Philippi to turn from worry by thinking instead about good, pure, and noble things. "Then the God of peace will be with you" (Philippians 4:6-9).

Not the other way around. Think peace first. By faith. Invite peace in. By faith. Walk in peace. By faith. Then the God of peace makes His empowered presence our blessed reward.

The war is over.
JERRY BRIDGES

Patience with Church

*So accept each other just as Christ has
accepted you; then God will be glorified.*

ROMANS 15:7

Even in church, not all people get along. No
surprise, in the fledgling church at Rome, Jews
and Gentiles were tense factions. So the apostle Paul
wrote them one letter. A tough letter. Tough to write.
Tough to read.

Tougher to swallow.

But be patient with each other, Paul wrote.

Patient with somebody who eats the "wrong" food?
Pays the "wrong" taxes? Believes the wrong kind of
gospel?

Exactly, Paul wrote. So be patient. "For even
Christ didn't live to please himself" (v. 3). Christ's self-
denial, with His sacrificial love on our behalf, is our
example, Paul added.

"So accept each other just as Christ has accepted
you." Look at the blessing. "Then God will be glorified" (v. 7).

We think that patience is a gift we give others,
period.

However, according to Paul, our patience for others in church glorifies God, reminding outsiders that God is great. Or as Paul said in verse 5, "May God, who gives this patience and encouragement, help you live in complete harmony with each other."

What a gift. *Complete harmony.* Indeed, what a promise. A church that demonstrates complete harmony is a living advertisement for the glory of God. *Look what God can do!* He can empower people who probably shouldn't get along to work together. "Each with the attitude of Christ Jesus toward the other" (v. 5).

Is patience easy? Of course not. The root of the word, the Latin *patiens*, means to suffer. In hospitals, the suffering are called just that—the patients. Yet we can pray for God to bless us with the patience to forbear others, just as Christ forbears us. Thus, let us pray for patience for one reason only—so God gets all the glory. What do we get? The blessing of beautiful harmony.

Have patience with all things, but chiefly have patience with yourself.
Francis de Sales

12

Patience under Pressure

*We give great honor to those who
endure under suffering.*
JAMES 5:11

Doctors called it impossible. Four weeks after a Haitian shop clerk was buried alive during a crushing earthquake, he was pulled alive from the rubble of the marketplace where he worked. His feet suffered wounds, and he was severely dehydrated and malnourished. Otherwise, he was fine. Expected to fully recover.

"This is just unbelievable," Dr. Barth Green, a Miami neurosurgeon who cofounded Project Medishare for Haiti, told reporters, "because to our knowledge, nobody has ever survived this long and the rescue efforts were called off almost two weeks ago."

What made the difference? "His family never gave up," Dr. Green said. His mother confirmed just that. "I stayed strong. I thought that I would find him."

Patience? Or a miracle? Or both? How else to explain the unidentified person "giving me water," as the man told doctors? In any case, the man kept waiting for help. Patient and believing.

It's the way we can wait. Believing God will move. Believing prayers will be answered. Letting the Holy Spirit empower our waiting with stubborn confidence, grit, and faith. Why, indeed, shouldn't we wait that way?

Patience under pressure. It is honorable, wrote James, the brother of Jesus. He was encouraging those in the early church at Jerusalem who were eager for the Lord's return.

But keep enduring, James urged, and his words still speak today. As the relief doctor in Haiti said of the patient clerk, "I think he's set a world record. . . . It'll be quite a story when fully told."

So it can be with us. Let it be said that we didn't give up on God. Not this generation. While others fainted, we failed not. Not today. Not tomorrow. Not forever.

When a man has quietly made up his mind that there is nothing he cannot endure, his fears leave him.
GROVE PATTERSON

Forgiven by God

*I show this unfailing love . . . by forgiving
every kind of sin and rebellion.*

Exodus 34:7

The girls in the jail were excited but subdued. It was their GED graduation day. But as teenage felons, they weren't graduating from jail. Most still had months, and some years, left to serve for their serious crimes. As their graduation speaker, what could I possibly say that would fit the occasion but also match their reality?

After praying and asking the Holy Spirit for help—especially since public speaking is its own challenge—I was intrigued when the perfect topic for my speech came to mind. Forgiveness.

My aim? To show the power of forgiveness to heal so we can move on. So I told the Bible story about Jesus and the lame man at the healing pool at Bethesda. One day, after the man had been lying there for thirty-eight years, Jesus asked him, "Would you *like* to get well?" (John 5:6, italics added). I wanted to show, first, that seeking forgiveness is a choice—that to forgive an old hurt or to forgive oneself is also like saying to Jesus, "Yes! I *would* like to be healed." Also, however, I sought to assure the girls in lockup that God forgives sin. Every kind of sin.

As I shared about God's healing forgiveness, many in the audience—girls, parents, and administrators—wiped away tears. It seemed the Holy Spirit was blessing us all with the reminder to forgive ourselves. So I closed with a gentle dare: "Look in the mirror tonight," I said. "Then tell yourself *you are forgiven.*" God loves you, I added. It was time now to move on.

A few weeks later I got an envelope of thank-you letters from the girls. "I really needed to hear this," one girl wrote. "I even told my sister about it." Many said similar things. The whole experience reminded me that, when it comes to forgiveness, the first thing to know—whether we seek forgiveness or whether we need to forgive—is that God forgives first. Every kind of sin. My worst. Your worst. He wants to bless you and me that way today.

Will you let Him? As you answer yes, you will bless His Spirit with your love.

> *Your own sins, no matter how big, are not bigger than God's pleasure in forgiveness.*
> EDWARD T. WELCH

Forgiveness: For God

*For the honor of your name, O LORD,
forgive my many, many sins.*

PSALM 25:11

I grew up black in the fifties—and Jim Crow was alive and well. So in the South, while visiting family, I couldn't sit in seats on the main floor of movie theaters, try on clothing and shoes in department stores, drink from water fountains with signs that shouted "Whites Only"—and I couldn't dream. Hate stops it.

So in return, I hated in reply. Even as a church-going Christian from birth, I thought all white people were bad. I tried hard to convince myself, anyway.

Years later, however, in my forties, the clogging burden of unforgiveness overwhelmed me. Desperate for healing, I sought the Lord's help in learning to forgive. It was cathartic, of course. Releasing burdens feels luxurious. We breathe better when we're forgiven. We breathe even better, however, when we forgive.

But why does God provide such an amazing gift? To mere human beings—who can remember the past with all its hurts and wrongs but can't change any of it—why would a Holy God offer this divine remedy called forgiveness? So we can feel better? In fact, yes.

But a greater reason prevails.

God forgives because it blesses and glorifies Him. The psalmist affirms it: "For the honor of your name, O LORD, forgive my many, many sins." God's reputation, that is, is elevated by the fact that He forgives. But also, when we forgive others, God is glorified—by our obedience and by our love.

A popular bumper sticker on the cars of countless Christians simply states it with one word: *Forgiven*. In my own life, forgiving racial wounds blessed and changed my life. But forgiving others, as some have told me, blessed and changed them more. Still, the healing wasn't just for us. When we forgive, it counts most for God.

> *Evangelism and reconciliation are*
> *two sides of the same message.*
> BRENDA SALTER MCNEIL

Forgiveness: For Love

*Love prospers when a fault is forgiven,
but dwelling on it separates close friends.*

PROVERBS 17:9

They sit at long tables on folding chairs. Many
are crying. As mothers of murdered children,
they bear pain too deep to imagine. Living in a
gang-ravaged neighborhood, they witness ongoing
violence as still more children die. Moreover, at every
turn, they are pressured to forgive. Some can't do it.

"It's too hard," one young mother sobs. "My *son
is dead*. He'll never walk this earth again. I know the
Lord says forgive, but why should I forgive *that*?"

Her question, asked in the fellowship hall of a
Denver church, cuts the atmosphere like a knife. I've
come to try to talk about forgiveness. But this is no
casual discussion group. These mothers hurt. To the
core. Why, indeed, should they forgive?

When it is my turn to talk, I dare to try to offer
some key reasons. That forgiveness is not about the
person who hurts us—not at first, anyway. That we
forgive to get healed. Then, when we're ready, God

offers His amazing remedy. Forgiveness. As important, however, we forgive *for* God—especially to reconnect with God. So forgiveness blesses God—showing we trust God enough to handle the injustice of the awful thing that happened. Then we move on, to serving God and blessing His Kingdom.

Oh, I prayed this was right.

I believe it is. As the late theologian Lewis Smedes writes in his beautiful book *The Art of Forgiving*, "As we start on the miracle of forgiving, we begin to see our enemy through a cleaner lens, less smudged by hate. We begin to see a real person . . . a human being created to be a child of God."

Will we become close friends with the person who wronged us? Only God knows. But either way, with forgiveness, we *will* renew our friendship with God. And what a beautiful friend. His love is too precious for any hurt to come between His Spirit and ours.

Forgiveness brings great joy, not only to the forgiven, but especially to the forgiver.
PHILIP GRAHAM RYKEN

Gratitude in Our Hearts

*One of them, when he saw that he
was healed, came back to Jesus.*

LUKE 17:15-16·

Ten lepers. All healed by Jesus. Yet only one came
back to say thank you. But why?

What made the one turn back to say thank you
to the Healing Christ? And why not the other nine?

Scholars have written volumes on this provocative scenario.

Charles Spurgeon writes that to neglect to thank
God for answered prayer "is to refuse to benefit
ourselves." Gratitude to God promotes the growth
of spiritual life, he adds. "It helps to remove our
burdens, to excite our hope, to increase our faith."
Other people get the benefit, too, when we show
gratitude to God. "Weak hearts will be strengthened,
and drooping saints will be revived as they listen to
our 'songs of deliverance.'"

Certainly this is right. But what about those nine?

Clearly, they felt compelled to go, as Jesus
instructed, to show themselves obediently to their

priests. They were more worried, apparently, about getting religious approval than blessing the one who'd approved them for healing. We see this, says John Reed, about the nine lepers, when "the spiritual razzmatazz becomes more significant than the converts' ongoing relationship with Christ."

C. S. Lewis notes that the healing itself took precedence over the Healer.

With the tenth leper, however, the Healer mattered more than the cure. As self-centered as most of us are, it's quite easy to forget to say thank you, even to God. The exception is when God means more to us than anything else—church rules, other people's opinions, expected blessings, and even our own delight in answered prayer.

Far better to delight in Him. He changes hearts. That's what healed the tenth leper. A new heart. The blessing? An empowered new life.

Gratitude is when memory is stored in the heart.
LIONEL HAMPTON

Gratitude for the Good

Enter his gates with thanksgiving.
PSALM 100:4

America's first Thanksgiving? Some say it was that December day in 1619 when a group of British settlers, led by Captain John Woodlief at Berkeley Plantation, Virginia, knelt in prayer and pledged "thanksgiving" to God for their safe arrival after a frightful voyage across the Atlantic.

Others cite that harvest meal in 1621 when the Pilgrims, after a brutal first year in the New World, celebrated a plentiful bounty—enough food to store and keep them alive through the coming winter. They were at peace, as well, with the native Indians. So Governor William Bradford, their leader, pro-claimed a day of thanksgiving shared by colonists and neighboring Indians alike.

Still other ceremonies of thanks have been recorded among settlers in North America—including Native Americans who observed harvest celebrations of thanks long before colonists or anybody else arrived.

What is the common denominator? And what do these thanksgivings teach us?

God deserves to be thanked—and should be. But taking time to bless Him with our thanks blesses us, too. We gather together. We circle a table. We pause to reflect on the countless marvelous things God does and provides every minute—from our next meal to our next breath—then we take time to savor it all.

The one hundredth psalm unveils it like this: "Enter his gates with thanksgiving; go into his courts with praise. Give thanks to him and bless his name" (v. 4). Any way we say it, however, God is blessed to hear it. Just as we're blessed to say it. So open your mouth right now and shout in your spirit: *Thank You, God!*

As the Lord loveth a cheerful giver,
so likewise a cheerful thanksgiver.
JOHN BOYS

Hope in God

Put your hope in the LORD.
Travel steadily along his path.
He will honor you by giving you the land.

PSALM 37:34

We were saving money. So we said no to adding a GPS for our rental car. But soon we were lost—despite two sets of directions. One was a map from the Internet. The other was hand-drawn directions from our hotel desk clerk, showing a "better" route. "Faster," she said, even though we were only going a few miles. Yet, my husband and I still got lost, unable to figure our way through a maze of unfamiliar streets in a town we didn't know.

One hour later, after several phone calls and several wrong turns—and more than one false start—we found our destination. It was right where the map said it would be, except for one problem. We'd traveled the wrong path.

Hoping for a faraway desire can seem like that—as if we're navigating a maze, and a destination, with no end in sight.

In the Scriptures, however, the psalmist exhorts us to hope in the Lord *and* travel steadily along *His* path. Then He will honor us by giving us the territory we desire.

Hope is not an idle pursuit. While we hope in the Lord for a desired outcome, we'll shorten our wait time by sticking to God's path. By the things we do. By the way we live. By the way we walk. Day by day. Thus, hoping in God means that while I wait on Him, I'll work on elevating my life, determining to be more like Him.

Too many of us think hope is enough in itself. But godly hope means walking in a higher way. On higher ground. As Andrew Murray notes about hopes expressed in prayer, "My prayer [hopes] will depend on my life." So move today from hoping to achieving. How? Stick to God's path. God will bless your sticking by delivering the beautiful outcome that lines up with Him.

If you do not hope, you will not find
what is beyond your hopes.
SAINT CLEMENT OF ALEXANDRIA

Hope despite Gloom and Trouble

*In my distress I prayed to the LORD,
and the LORD answered me and rescued me.*

PSALM 118:5

The woman's mother was depressed. Clinically depressed. And it baffled her. Once the "fun" mom among her friends' mothers—the one who found fun things to do on rainy days, drove them as children to picnics and swim parties, loved silly jokes, and told funny stories—her mother now spent her days curled up in a chair. Refusing to go anywhere. Refusing to get dressed. Refusing to live her life.

But her daughter clung to hope.

After seeking God in prayer for answers—and pressing her mother's doctor for relief—a treatment plan emerged: A change in her mother's medicines. An improved diet. Exercise. Psychotherapy. Morning and evening prayer. And sunlight.

In their gloomy Midwest-winter environment, her mother was prescribed a half-hour regimen of "full-spectrum" light therapy from a lamp that simulated the sunlight her mother was missing. Over time, with the combination of treatments, her mother's depression started to lift. But none of this would have happened, this woman insists, if she had not first sought God with hope. "I was at the end of my rope," she says. "My mother was miserable, and so was I." So, like the psalmist, she prayed to the Lord, and the Lord answered. *Get up with hope—then take your mother to the doctor!*

Get up in the dark, that is. Even when you can't see any hope. Even when you can't imagine that a hopeful resolution is even possible. *Get up anyway.* In distress, get up with hope. Then, in that darkness, God sees and God hears and God answers. "We could still be sitting in the dark, feeling lost and hopeless," this woman says. Instead, she let distress stir her failing hope. She let distress force her to stand up. She let distress jump-start her feeble plea. Then the faithful God responded. Our distress doesn't scare God, in other words. Our distress softens His ear. Then as we pray, He answers. How? With the bright and beautiful blessing of hope.

Hope is patience with the lamp lit.
TERTULLIAN

20

Thrift That Maximizes My Giving

*For God is the one who provides seed for the
farmer and then bread to eat. In the same way,
he will provide and increase your resources and
then produce a great harvest of generosity in you.*

2 CORINTHIANS 9:10

When Paul taught this lesson on giving,
he spoke of farming and seed stock and
harvest—all concepts that meant something real to
first-century Christians. His teaching can feel rele-
vant to believers today, as well, if we listen closely.

Giving back money to God surely can challenge
the best of us, especially if we're not living by biblical
principles of thrift and money management, so our
money supply always seems tight. But Paul offered
this smart reminder: Farmers always keep back a
portion of seed from each harvest to plant for next
year's crop.

The tithe operates the same way. Giving back to
God that 10 percent off the top of our earnings—our

firstfruits—shows Him to be our Provider of it all, the one alone who increases our resources in order to "produce a great harvest of generosity."

As Paul wrote to the Corinthians, "the one who plants generously will get a generous crop" (2 Corinthians 9:6). But don't give reluctantly or under pressure. "For God loves a person who gives cheerfully" (v. 7). Or as Crown Financial Ministries, the Christian money-management organization, says about such matters: "The principle of tithing is centered on the fact that God is looking for the right attitude in a person's giving." Any distraction over the percentage misses the point. God doesn't own just the 10 percent; He owns the 90 percent left over, too. So as you and I tithe, let's pray over all of it.

And if you're in deep debt and tithing only 1 or 2 percent until you can give more, keep tithing cheerfully. Your attitude is what counts. Then watch your ability to earn *and* to give grow in kind. "Then you will always have everything you need," Paul said, "and plenty left over to share with others" (v. 8). And your harvest? As it grows, watch it glorify God.

It is a matter of the heart in giving to God.
CROWN FINANCIAL MINISTRIES

21

Praise That Shakes Things Up

Suddenly, there was a great earthquake.
ACTS 16:26

Don't wait. Not a minute. Not a second. Instead, praise God now. If you and I wait to praise God until *after* something earthshaking and amazing happens, we've got the wrong order. Praise comes first. Doubt that?

Consider the classic praise story in the Bible—this scenario where Paul and Silas, bound in chains in the dungeon of a jail, their bodies bruised and bloodied by their jailers, still lifted their voices to praise God.

And what an odd sound. Praise in a jail. Sung by two beaten, bloodied prisoners. It's not logical. But as the book of Acts records, as they praised God, the earth shook. "And the prison was shaken to its foundations. All the doors flew open, and the chains of every prisoner fell off!" (v. 26). Praise is power, indeed. But *praise comes first*.

When we're bound up by some situation, in the midst of that mess, it's hard to remember that we should praise God first. Not after it's all cleaned up. But while it's happening. That is the proper order of praise.

In fact, the word *praise* (which in Latin means "prize") shares a root with the Latin word for preposition. As we recall from grammar lessons at school, a preposition is the word that comes *before* the main thing. Such words hold the "before" position—the *pre*position—setting up the main topic. In our spiritual lives, praise sits in that same place. It holds the *pre*position, setting up God's power so it can follow, moving in our hearts and lives.

And no prison chains can tie down that power. So don't wait for your chains to fall or your prison walls to crumble. Praise God *first*. Right now. Despite your circumstances. Praise Him for being God. For His mercy. For His deliverance. For His hope. For His blessing. For His beautiful, empowering Spirit. Then stand back. Your prison walls are coming down!

---

*Some think that worship is a response
after the Holy Spirit moves upon them.
However, it's the other way around.*
Dale A. Robbins

22

Praise with Power

And the chains of every prisoner fell off!
ACTS 16:26

*E*very prisoner in the jail was freed? Does that get your attention today? *Every* prisoner freed. An amazing detail in this story of the apostle Paul's praise meeting in a grungy, bloodstained jailhouse with Silas.

Those faithful men prayed and praised God— so it's no surprise that God loosed the chains of these two. But, *in addition*, every other prisoner bound in that cold and dingy jail got freed. As their praise shook that jail, *all* the chains on *every* prisoner flat out fell off!

Maybe, like me, you'd forgotten this little detail: that our feeble but faithful praise can prompt God to loose, not just our chains, but the chains of others around us.

So, in church, get on your feet and praise the Lord! Somebody in the next pew might catch the fire and find his or her chains loosed too.

In your family, open your mouth and praise Him.

Somebody sitting around your kitchen table—or in your family tree, or on your Facebook page, or in your Twitter feed—might find his or her own spiritual bindings unraveling. Why? Because God is good and *you* praised God.

It's an amazing and supernatural phenomenon. In this story, in fact, even the jailer experienced freedom. Realizing the freed prisoners had not bolted and escaped, he called out: "Sirs, what must I do to be saved?" (Acts 16:30).

"Believe on the Lord Jesus," Paul and Silas replied, "and you will be saved, *along with your entire household*" (v. 31, italics added).

Praising God is contagious! Supernaturally.

God's Spirit alone could make it so—this remarkable principle that *my* praise can cause *your* soul to be freed, blessed, and delivered. Yes, praise is an additive. Let it overflow your heart, freeing someone else's life on this God-given day.

We increase whatever we praise.
CHARLES FILLMORE

23

Praise: Into His Presence

O thou that inhabitest the praises of Israel . . .
PSALM 22:3, KJV

A gloomy Sunday? Sometimes they hit. So I dragged myself to church and sank into my pew. Feeling empty. Feeling angry. Feeling lethargic. A family matter weighed heavy on my heart. My arms felt like lead weights. Lift them to praise? I couldn't manage it—not on my own. Not on this Sunday. That's what the enemy wanted me to think. But I clung to a Scripture verse I've heard all my life—that God inhabits, or enthrones Himself, in the praises of His people. That when we praise Him, our praise lifts us into His comforting, uplifting, empowering, strengthening, invigorating presence.

So I opened my mouth. Wide. I started to sing along with the choir's praise song. *Thank You, Lord! Thank You, Lord! I just want to thank You, Lord!*

As the words left my mouth, I could feel my arms rise from my sides. As they rose, I thought—in particular—about the many ways the Lord has blessed me, my family members, my church, my work, my friends, my neighborhood, my nation, our world, because of who He is.

In fact, I closed my eyes, recalling my older daughter's recent acceptance into a prestigious graduate school, my younger daughter and her husband's announcement that their next baby would be a healthy little boy, my husband's recovery from a major medical crisis, the merciful pain relief from my own shoulder injury—and more. In fact, the more I praised, the more I was flooded with images of how great and good God is.

In moments, I was moved from my emotional emptiness to a celebration of rejoicing at God's goodness. Or as my pastor declared: "Can't you feel it? Feel God's presence in this house today?" I nodded—tentatively. Could I feel His presence? Not in the sanctuary, I decided. But I *could* feel His presence in my heart, enthroned on my praise. And what a feeling. It felt comforting, strong, protective, powerful. Loving. Yes, my praise gave God a place in my heart to stand up and stay. Unmovable.

Praise is the honey of life.
CHARLES SPURGEON

24

Faith That Glorifies God

*Didn't I tell you that you would see
God's glory if you believe?*

JOHN 11:40

Lazarus was dead. Stone-cold dead. In the grave four days. As dead as some of our dreams. More dead than many of our hopes. He was so dead that his sister Martha, though distressed that Jesus hadn't arrived soon enough to keep him alive, feared to open his grave. It would smell, she said. A "terrible" smell, she insisted (v. 39).

The smell of death is foul, to be sure.

When dreams die—and things don't turn out as we'd hoped, but sometimes much worse—the stench of our disappointment can befoul our entire lives. Looking back, all we see is the grungy brokenness of our upended desires.

Worse, our "friends" follow behind us, questioning our God. "This man healed a blind man. Why couldn't he keep [your dream] from dying?"

Jesus' answer presents a sharp rebuttal to such smelly circumstances.

The unraveling of a beloved dream—or a life plan or lifetime goal—may appear to be a total and irreversible disaster. Bankruptcy. Sickness. Divorce. Job loss. Theft. Murder. War. All are horrible, for certain. But they don't have to end in irreversible death.

"No, it is for the glory of God," Jesus said. "I, the Son of God, will receive glory from this" (v. 4). Or as he told Martha, "Those who believe in me, even though they die like everyone else, will live again. They are given eternal life for believing in me and will never perish" (vv. 25-26).

Lazarus was raised from death by Christ. But we who believe also are raised from the death, disillusionment, and deception of dashed dreams. We can bemoan our losses. Or we can believe that God will revive us as we walk by faith from death to new life, for His glory. Yesterday *is* dead. But today? Look with faith to God for the beautiful blessing of future life.

Never be afraid to trust an unknown future to a known God.
CORRIE TEN BOOM

25

Faith That Makes Miracles

Anything is possible if a person believes.
MARK 9:23

Jesus' disciples are in a quandary in this story. A sick boy's father has begged them to cast out an evil spirit from his son. But no go. They can't do it.

Then Jesus shows up. In His presence, the evil spirit goes berserk—throwing the boy into a violent convulsion, leaving him writhing on the ground and foaming at the mouth. A disturbing scene. A big problem. Or as the boy's father puts it: "Have mercy on us and help us. Do something if you can" (v. 22).

If He can?

Jesus is bemused. "What do you mean, 'If I can?'"

Jesus questions the extraordinary suggestion that perhaps He can't cast out the ungodly spirits in our lives. Jesus can't? It's absurd. Yet, like the boy's father, we doubt Him. So Jesus turns the tables, challenging the father: "Anything is possible if a person believes" (v. 23). Now *that's* an extraordinary suggestion. Jesus can. If *I* can.

It's a theological principle that challenges the best

of us. Or as the boy's father says: "I do believe, but help me not to doubt!" (v. 24).

We need to say that today. Help, O God, my unbelief. My uncertainty. My need for proof. Help me to stop stumbling over my human obstacles and to focus, not on problems, but on Your divine ability to accomplish anything, including what looks impossible.

In this story, in fact, as a crowd gathers around, Jesus casts out the evil spirit, demanding that it never enter the boy again. By His power? Absolutely. But that power was kindled by a feeble man's faith. Like yours. Like mine. So stop struggling today with feeble faith. Confess your doubts. But count on God. His Spirit will transform that doubt into a blessing of faith. Why? Because He can.

Faith takes God without any ifs.
D. L. MOODY

26

Faith That Empowers Prayer

*If you believe, you will receive
whatever you ask for in prayer.*
MATTHEW 21:22, NIV

It's controversial, this promise that Jesus made—
that if we just believe when we ask, we will receive
what we ask. But it doesn't work, say those whose
circumstances haven't changed. Perhaps they are
missing the real lesson.

That odd lesson, yes, when Jesus first curses a fig
tree for sprouting only leaves.

"May you never bear fruit again!" he declares
(v. 19). And immediately, the Scripture reports, the
fig tree withers and dies. The disciples, amazed, start
questioning Jesus about why the fig tree withered
so quickly.

But Jesus answers by teaching—that if we have
faith and believe, we can do such things. ("You can
even say to this mountain, 'May God lift you up and
throw you into the sea,' and it will happen," v. 21).

Then Jesus adds: "If you believe, you will receive
whatever you ask for in prayer" (v. 22, NIV).

From figs to prayer? It seems an odd way to teach a lesson on faith. So some scholars say Jesus was targeting hypocrisy—in "religious" people who put on the outer appearance of being fruitful, as fruitful as a fig tree, but aren't fruitful at all. Others say Jesus was making a point about faithless Israel, a nation professing to be faithful to God, but often failing to obey Him.

Either way, the larger point seems to be about the role of faith in our lives: that those who walk in faith can do what seems impossible. Our faith shapes our prayers, that is, but also our lives. So if we believe our answer is coming, we act like it. Even before we see it. Across the ages, legions of Christians have doubted this, based on their circumstances. But this Bible story shows that the blessing of answered prayer doesn't depend on circumstances. Answered prayer rests, instead, on blessing God with our faith. Then we watch God's Spirit beautifully bless us with a harvest.

Beware in your prayer, above everything, of limiting God.
ANDREW MURRAY

27

Joy with Strength

For the joy of the LORD is your strength!
NEHEMIAH 8:10

She's laughing. Even though her home is a wreck.
She's laughing. Even though her project looks
lousy. Paint colors all wrong. Fabric choices too
costly. When the kitchen cabinets finally arrive—
several weeks late—both the size and wood grain
completely miss the mark.

"But I'm laughing," says the TV host of the home
renovation show, giggling into the camera. "It's how
I deal with setbacks," she explains. "I mean, you *have*
to laugh. It gets me back on track."

It's a timeless philosophy. Joy imparts strength.

For believers, however, joy in the Lord activates
His strength. In our lives. In our circumstances. In
our projects. Both big and small.

Speaking to His disciples, Jesus put it this way:
"Here on earth you will have many trials and sorrows.
But take heart"—be of good cheer—"because I have
overcome the world" (John 16:33). We love that
promise, indeed.

But why should joy in Him—and not courage or bravery or boldness—deliver the strength of almighty God? Could it be the illogic of the principle? That the beauty of joy is so winsome that it's disarming?

No enemy expects a foe to fight back *with joy.*

Yet there's something strangely powerful about joy. About laughing in the face of a storm. About sizing up your enemy but knowing that, compared to God, your enemy is powerless. About staring up at a mountain and assessing its peaks, crags, and valleys, but knowing—as you laugh—the mountain can't overcome God's power. Is this rationalizing? Or denial? Or is it wisdom?

"I have told you this so that you will be filled with my joy," Jesus told His disciples in the upper room (John 15:11). "Yes, your joy will overflow!" Then as His joy flows, your enemies flee. Can you laugh at that? Try it today. Your victory will follow.

Joy comes to your rescue—if you let it.
BONNIE ST. JOHN

28

Joy: Doubled

*Well done, thou good and faithful servant.
. . . Enter thou into the joy of thy lord.*
MATTHEW 25:21, KJV

Want to know what God expects from us? Not a little. Not a lot. Double. Yes, twice what God gives us in His blessings, He wants double that back. A lot to ask? Not when we consider what He longs to give us in return:

Yet more life. More blessings. More joy. *His* joy.

More than we can contain. More than we can imagine.

Not so our enemy.

"The thief's purpose is to steal and kill and destroy," Jesus says of Satan, but also of any enemy that robs us of His joy (John 10:10). But what is the purpose of Christ? "I am come that they might have life, and that they might have it more abundantly" (KJV).

He explains how in the story of the three servants. All three received money from their master, but in differing amounts. Right away, the first servant got busy investing his money—and doubled it. The second servant did the same—doubling his amount. Both earned their master's praise. "Well done!" They also both got job promotions. "I will give you many more responsibilities" (Matthew 25:21). Best of all, however, they were invited to celebrate, sharing their master's joy.

To share their master's strength, that is. Abundantly. And, yes, such a beautiful blessing comes with a price. That price can never compare, however, with the price Christ paid on the cross for our joy. Double His benefits? In truth, we should be willing to give back even more—because it all belongs to Him anyway.

The third servant learned that the hard way. Fearful, he dug a hole and hid his master's money so he wouldn't lose it. But he lost much more. He lost his master's joy. Want a different outcome? Get up and get busy for Christ, empowered by God's Spirit. Your blessing? Your Master's joy.

The most precious truth in the Bible is that God's greatest interest is to glorify the wealth of His grace by making sinners happy in Him.
JOHN PIPER

29

Joy with Obedient Love

*When you obey me . . . you will be filled
with my joy. Yes, your joy will overflow!*
JOHN 15:10-11

The path to obeying Christ is no mystery. He high-
lighted only two commandments. Both focus on
love. And we know the two commandments well. Love
God with all our hearts, souls, and minds. And love
our neighbors as ourselves (see Matthew 22:37-39).

Discussing such love in the upper room,
however, Jesus further explained the benefits of
obeying Him in these matters. In short, we find joy.

"When you obey me, you remain in my love,"
Jesus said, "just as I obey my Father and remain in
his love." Then He added: "I have told you this so
that you will be filled with my joy. Yes, your joy will
overflow!"

There is great blessing, Jesus was saying, in doing
what God asks. And what He asks is simple. Love
Me. Love our neighbors.

We could complicate all of this—and we often
do. One young man even asked Jesus to explain,

exactly, who is a "neighbor." You may recall Jesus then told the story of the Good Samaritan, featuring so-called good people—including a priest—who stepped around an injured man rather than get involved to help him.

It's not the Good Samaritan that Jesus mentioned, however, when He gathered with His disciples in the upper room, the night before His crucifixion— that night before the day when everything in the universe changed. On that night, Jesus talked not about gloomy, horrible, torturous things. Instead, He washed His disciples' feet, encouraging them to follow His mandate to love. Why? "So that you will be filled with my joy." Well, more than filled. By loving, we will overflow with joy. Silly sometimes with joy. Then we will rest with joy.

Those who make following Christ a long laundry list of dos and don'ts—or *thou shalts* and *thou shalt nots*—might instead be refreshed by returning to the upper room. There, Jesus offers us a simple prescription. Take His love and give it back. In exchange, He blesses with joy.

The religion of Christ is the religion of joy.
OCTAVIUS WINSLOW

Hospitality: By Faith

*So there was food every day for Elijah
and for the woman and her family.*

1 KINGS 17:15, NIV

Feed strangers? On *my* budget? Perhaps you've struggled, as I have, with the challenge of sharing hospitality when your own cupboard feels bare. That excuse fizzles when we recall the widow of Zarephath—so poor and bereft she was gathering sticks to cook her last meal "that we may eat it—and die" (v. 12, NIV).

But the prophet Elijah shows up with a pep talk. "Don't be afraid" (v. 13, NIV). Always a good word. But he also wants food. Specifically, *her* meager food.

Still, by faith, she obeys—going to her hovel to make up a small cake of bread for Elijah from her last handful of flour and last drops of oil. But, sure enough, as Elijah promises, there is food every day for Elijah and for the woman and her family. Why?

"For the jar of flour was not used up and the jug of oil did not run dry, in keeping with the word of the LORD spoken by Elijah" (v. 16, NIV).

That same word is spoken to us today. In short, regardless of how much—or how little—we have in our homes to share with others, we are commanded to give. And just look at the benefit. When we share by faith, as the widow at Zarephath shared, God restores and multiplies what He's blessed us with in the first place. And no, this never should be the purpose of our hospitality—to be rewarded by God with more.

Yet that's the outcome. In the book *Making Room* on reviving Christian hospitality, author Christine Pohl describes the ways hospitable Christians get blessed—from sensing God's presence to finding new friends. With more friends, it's hard to run out of resources, spiritually or practically. In fact, when the widow's son gets sick and dies, her guest Elijah prays to God, asking Him to restore to life the boy whose mother "has opened her home to me" (v. 20).

Her blessing shouldn't surprise us. Her boy lived.

*Good hosts discover . . . they are themselves
beloved guests of God's grace.*
CHRISTINE POHL

Reverence and Fear of God: For Our Prosperity

Who are those who fear the LORD? . . . They will live in prosperity, and their children will inherit the land.

PSALM 25:12-13

My dad took no prisoners. He was tall and stern. A World War II veteran. Not given to foolishness. Not inclined to compromise. Not kidding around when it came to the things of family or things of God. He'd made a pact with God, as the story goes, that if he survived World War II—where he served for three years as an infantry unit commander in the South Pacific—he would serve Him all the days of his life.

Bargaining with God? I don't think so. But my dad kept his promises. So he was faithful to his wife, responsible for his children, devoted to his church, and fearful *only* of God. But something else.

My dad was prosperous. Materially, in fact, he did well—although not all who obey God succeed in this way. But as the Latin *pro spere* implies, my dad succeeded with favor, *according to his hope*. (*Spere* in Latin means "hope.") That is, Daddy feared and revered the God in whom he hoped and whom he feared.

Still, for my dad, prosperity wasn't about material success. As in the Hebrew definitions of prosperity—to journey well, to press on against great odds, to have wisdom, to enjoy peace and well-being—my dad's first goal was to prosper in his soul.

Despite a rocky road. As a young black veteran—a civil servant who worked thirty-plus years for the U.S. government, enduring the Jim Crow era and all manner of racial injustice and bias—my dad faced tough roadblocks. Surely, indeed, each of us faces our own rough challenges in life.

My dad taught me to overcome challenges, however, by fearing only God.

So he lived right. And he prospered—especially as God prospers us. Thus, instead of faltering, Daddy endured—aiming high, working hard, going far. Along the way, he taught his children about Jesus—surely our greatest inheritance, and his greatest legacy. You, too, can bless your children beautifully with such holy prosperity. How? Fear only God.

Those know enough who know how to fear God.
MATTHEW HENRY

32

Reverence and Fear of God with Great Abundance

True humility and fear of the LORD lead to riches.
PROVERBS 22:4

"Who's rich?"

The woman at the battered-women's shelter asked her question. Her good question. "It makes me smile to think about it," she said. "So I'll ask everybody here tonight—are you rich?"

None of us at this Bible study, in fact, was a wealthy fat cat—surely not in money. Of our small group, half the women were from my inner-city church. The others were residents of the shelter, all trying to find jobs, resettle with their children, and restart their lives. By our bank accounts, in truth, some could be called "poor."

Yet we all raised our hands. Or as one young woman said, "I *know* I'm rich."

She explained: "I have life in my body. Air in my lungs. Joy in my heart. Salvation in Christ. I look out at the beautiful day and I can see it. So yes— I *am* rich!"

A perfect answer. A godly answer. To be sure, the Bible sometimes speaks of riches as a blessing from God—as in Proverbs 8:18. Other Scriptures, however, warn against hoarding riches or trusting in riches instead of God. So Psalm 62:10 makes it plain: "If your wealth increases, don't make it the center of your life."

Jesus stresses the same, noting, "How hard it is for the rich to enter the Kingdom of God!" (Mark 10:23).

At this humble women's shelter, likewise, our friend's question provoked us to see with new eyes God's promise that honoring Him may lead to material wealth.

For certain, fearing God leads to spiritual wealth. Without limits.

This abundance, built fearfully and humbly, relying on God's Spirit and His incomparable mercies, doesn't just make you and me rich. It is a treasure that is priceless.

The real measure of our wealth is how much we should be worth if we lost our money.
J. H. JOWETT

33

Obedience to the Son

"Follow me," Jesus said.
LUKE 5:27, NIV

As commands go, these two words of Jesus are plain and clear. But for me, on a cool, cloudy springtime afternoon, the words seemed complex and deep. I'd just returned from a meeting with my pastor—where I'd asked officially to be considered as a local deacon. I'd be on the path to ordination. But was I ready? Ready to follow Jesus *there*?

Such following challenges God's servants for two key reasons. First, if we stay too far behind the Lord—not drawing near to His Spirit—we never catch up to His ways, His deeds, His truth. Second, however, we can't follow if we don't know Him. In today's Scripture, the tax collector Levi—despite his crooked lifestyle—knew precisely who Jesus was. Jesus was Levi's path to a new life. At Christ's call, Levi "got up, left everything and followed" (v. 28, NIV).

What a contrast to the people of Nazareth. "Isn't this Joseph's son?" they asked. They were amazed, reports the Gospel of Luke, "at the gracious words that came from his lips." At first, in fact, they spoke well of Him (Luke 4:22, NIV). Then the tables turned. The people got sidetracked. They wanted Jesus to perform in Nazareth the miracles He had performed in Capernaum and elsewhere. Jesus' reply—"no prophet is accepted in his hometown"—revealed the true spirit of the Nazarenes (v. 24, NIV). True, they were intrigued by Joseph's returning son. But they were "furious" that He refused to perform deeds for them (v. 28). Not seeing His divinity, they tried to throw Him off a cliff.

Levi, instead, set off on a life-changing adventure with Jesus. At the word *follow*, he would understand its Hebrew essence—*halak,* meaning "walk," was like saying *walk with me.* It's what makes obedience to the Son such a blessing. Despite the challenge of walking with Christ—of obeying His call to go where He leads—something precious keeps us on the journey: No matter our ministry or mission, when we get up to travel with Jesus, we never walk alone.

Unless he obeys, a man cannot believe.
DIETRICH BONHOEFFER

34

Obedience in Plenty

*I will look on you with favor and make you
fruitful and increase your numbers.*

LEVITICUS 26:9, NIV

Like all Christians, I want God's favor. I long
for it, in fact. To be honest, I want not just to
be loved *and* liked by God. I want to be one of His
favorites—so much that He blesses me with fruitful-
ness for Him. *But also increases it.*

That may sound like a greedy, worldly, clawing
desire. As I commit to obeying Him, however, I find
my desires don't shrink—as some theologies suggest
they should. Instead, my desires expand. That's how
it should be. Obedient followers don't want less from
God. We *should* want more.

But not for ourselves. In obedience, we should
want more of God—*for* God—and for His people.

It follows that God offers, in return, exactly what
obedient followers crave. A great harvest. "You will
still be eating last year's harvest," the Lord promises
the obedient, when it's time to "make room for the
new" (Leviticus 26:10, NIV, italics added).

Such blessed extravagance! But as we read deeper into these verses, we are shown why. "I will look on you with favor . . . *and I will keep my covenant with you*," declares the Lord (v. 9, NIV, italics added). As obedient followers, our favorable status and our fruitful increase both witness to the world, not our greatness, but the faithfulness of our God.

Yes, the Maker of the covenant also keeps it. Those who see will understand exactly who He is: the Promise Maker *and* the Promise Keeper.

What a great lesson for believers longing for godly favor but never seeming to find it. The solution? Obedience. It should be assuring, in fact, to learn that God isn't arbitrary with favor and increase. *If* we follow His decrees, He says, we'll realize these blessings. For God, it is the perfect arrangement. He can give much to the obedient. Why? He knows we will give it away.

A great work is made out of a combination of obedience and liberty.
NADIA BOULANGER

35

Righteousness in Friendship

He offers his friendship to the godly.
PROVERBS 3:32

God wants to be our friend. An amazing truth. Too hard to believe? It could even be too hard to consider. But the Bible confirms His holy longing for friendship with His creation. Listen in Revelation 3:20 to Jesus: "Look! Here I stand at the door and knock. If you hear me calling and open the door, I will come in, and we will share a meal as friends."

Or ponder Abraham—who believed God, "so God declared him to be righteous," then he was called "the friend of God" (James 2:23).

In the upper room, meantime, Jesus told his disciples: "You are my friends if you do what I command. . . . I have called you friends, for everything that I learned from my Father I have made known to you. You did not choose me, but I chose you" (John 15:14-16, NIV).

Me? Amazing. But there is a condition to God's friendship.

We have to get up, by His grace, and act godly. By keeping in touch with God. Being trustworthy. Confiding in God. Obeying. Forgiving. Listening. Following through. Not just talking about being a friend, but acting like one. By sticking closer than a brother.

To be a real friend, in other words, requires our best. We try to take the high road. Sacrificing our own interests. And in that effort? God chooses us as His friends. Right here on earth.

Then look at the blessings. We can confide in Him. Enjoy His forgiveness. Share and listen. Sharpen our honesty, integrity, and truth. Then whatever righteousness we brought to the friendship grows even more. Are you enjoying His friendship this year? Stand up and say yes. Then let Him bless you with a priceless gift—the rightness of Him.

It is in relationships that we develop into what God wants us to be.
KENT HUGHES

36

Righteousness in Abundance

*He grants a treasure of good sense to
the godly. He is their shield.*
PROVERBS 2:7

I was a church girl, but not enough. So lacking
godliness in the deepest parts of my life, I lacked
what I needed most: common sense.

It doesn't come easy, indeed. Common sense
is developed. Often over a long lifetime, common
sense may finally settle in, giving those who employ
it a sense of command in life, a supply of good rea-
soning in decision making, and an air of favor where
others experience disdain or despair.

Common sense is worth its weight in gold, to be
sure. Or as the nineteenth-century American popu-
list Josh Billings put it: "Common sense is the knack
of seeing things as they are, and doing things as they
ought to be done."

But what if it didn't require a lifetime of experience to acquire such good sense?

In his writings, King Solomon of the Bible shows
how: follow God.

When we cry to God's Spirit, seeking to walk in His ways, God grants a treasury of good sense, Solomon promises. For godly people, that is, God's storehouse of grace and protection never runs out when it comes to common sense.

A priceless blessing, to be sure.

So, buy a piece of land near a vile swamp? Common sense says no. Marry a beautiful, rich woman with an evil, sharp tongue? Common sense says no. Wear a thin coat on a cold and bitter day? Common sense says no. Go into business with a known cheat? Common sense shouts *no*. We ignore common sense to our own peril, Solomon warns. When our desires, lusts, and egos get in the way, common sense loses out.

But trusting God enough to stand up for His ways over others' blesses us with the keys to one of God's greatest treasuries: His good sense. As you consider this priceless treasure, rise up today and choose right. Then watch blessings flow.

The voice of the Lord is the voice of common sense.
SAMUEL BUTLER

37

Humility with Strength

For when I am weak, then I am strong.
2 CORINTHIANS 12:10

Satan tricks us. Our enemy wants us to think humble people are losers. Thus, to us, humility can feel weak, passive, and wimpy. We're conditioned by our culture, in fact, to see meekness and mildness as nerdy and negative.

God's Word repeatedly tells us, however, how the Lord honors our honest nothingness. With His peace. With His inheritance. With His wisdom. With "riches, honor, and long life" (Proverbs 22:4).

Thus, John the Baptist's urgent longing that "He must become greater and greater, and I must become less and less" (John 3:30) only begins to capture the divine rewards in choosing lowly humility over self-preening pride.

To make it plain, God cares for the humble.

Why? The humble allow God to be God.

The apostle Paul—perhaps the most influential Christian in the history of the faith—reflected on the surrendering power of such humility. In Paul's second letter to the Corinthians, he described being given a "thorn in my flesh . . . to torment me" and "keep me from becoming proud." Three times, in fact, he begged the Lord to take this thorn away. But each time, the Lord told Paul: "My grace is all you need." Why?

"My power works best in weakness."

As Paul observed: "That's why I take pleasure in my weaknesses. . . . For when I am weak, then I am strong" (2 Corinthians 12:7-10).

Will you let the deep truth of this promise sink into your soul today? Perhaps you're not top dog in your circle. Or perhaps you were top dog, but you're laying down such vain ambition to walk humbly with God. Will you bless Him by trusting His promise—that He honors, cares for, and empowers the humble? If you will, get ready to experience more strength than you can ask for or imagine. For when you are meek and lowly and humble and weak, *He* is stronger.

God created the world out of nothing, and so long as we are nothing, He can make something out of us.
MARTIN LUTHER

38

Humility with Wisdom

With humility comes wisdom.
PROVERBS 11:2

I was a hotshot writer, or so I thought. Since grade school, awards and plaques covered my bedroom walls—largely due to strong scores in English and composition. Then I went to college.

My first papers earned only average grades. Lots of Cs. Far too many Cs, in fact. Then on a cloudy fall day, I held a paper in my hand with an F.

I stared at it. Holding back tears. Trying to listen to the professor. Forcing myself not to cry. Or scream. An *F*? For *me*? The high school honor student? It was all I could do not to crumple the paper in shreds and storm out of the classroom. Then I read the professor's note. The writing was fine, she wrote, but I'd made an error of fact. Result? An automatic F.

So I dried my eyes. I swallowed hard. Humility doesn't go down easy.

I approached the professor after class, thanking her for pointing out the mistake and vowing not to let it happen again. The next day, I visited another professor—asked him to review my mistakes. I asked to see some A-quality papers, to get a better idea of his standards. I swallowed hard as he shared "better" papers than mine. Then I listened hard as he explained why mine fell short. Then he showed me how to improve.

Humbling? Humbling beyond words.

But owning my mistakes and shortcomings, and asking for help to improve a skill I thought I'd already mastered, proved to be one of the wisest choices of my college years. Before long, I was earning As in both those classes. But even if I hadn't worked to raise my grades, the wisdom required to try came only after swallowing the hard pill of humility.

Do you lack wisdom in certain areas of your life? Can you swallow a hard pill? Ask the Holy Spirit to grant you a spirit of humility. God promises the beauty of wisdom will follow.

Humility is the mother of all virtues.
STEPHEN COVEY

39

Trust in His Way

*Trust in the LORD and do good. Then you
will live safely in the land and prosper.*

PSALM 37:3

Over his lifetime, King David stood up to
plenty of people doing bad. The giant Goliath,
of course. And King Saul, who tried to kill this
boy musician-turned-warrior. Then, after doing
bad himself—by fathering a baby with another
man's wife and having her husband killed—David
repented before God, but he and his family still
suffered the consequences. His son Amnon raped
David's daughter Tamar, who was Amnon's own half
sister. Tamar's brother Absalom murdered Amnon.
Later, Absalom waged war against David, seeking to
steal the throne while David was still alive.

Talk about doing bad and paying for it.

More than anybody in the Bible, indeed, David
had authority to write in Psalm 37 what he'd learned
the hard way: "Trust in the LORD." Not in yourself.
Not in your emotions. Not in your lusts. Not in
your shrewdness. One wonders, in fact: Did David

actually think having sex with a woman who wasn't his wife and murdering her husband would make things *good*?

Finally, he figured it out.

Trust in the LORD. But that's not all. *Do good.*

That's another way of saying, do what God wills. That is, do what God commands. Do what God teaches. Do what God requires.

Don't know what *good* is? Or what God commands? Then let's spend time with God. Fellowship with God. Study God's Word. Quiet our own interests. Instead, let's seek God to learn His way. Then what happens?

David explained clearly. "Then you will live safely in the land." But that's not all. Those who trust in the Lord—*and* do good—live safely in the land *and they prosper.*

Is there any reason to doubt it? Trust Him today and see.

If God has said it, it will be so.
CHARLES SPURGEON

40

Trust: In Full

*Even strong young lions sometimes go hungry, but
those who trust in the LORD will lack no good thing.*

PSALM 34:10

Among the cat family, lions are the only social
breed. Living in large groups called prides, these
families of about fifteen lions are made up mostly of
related females and their young. The male lion doesn't
hang around long. Within prides, as such, the female
lions are affectionate, showing lots of touching, head
rubbing, licking, and purring. Hunting mostly at
night, the females work in teams to stalk and ambush
their prey, bringing down food for their young.

Thus, it's *very* unusual for a young lion in a pride
to go hungry.

But even a strong, beloved lion might miss a
meal sometimes.

As a shepherd boy, David—the author of this
psalm—would know that well. He fought off bears
and lions, learning their ways and habits in order to
protect his sheep.

But he also learned the ways of God, in whom
David trusted. So he learned that, with God, he

never lacked good things. Courage. Skill. Wisdom. God provided enough, always.

Young lions couldn't claim that. As pampered and well fed and petted as they were, they'd go hungry sometimes. Their mothers failed to find food sometimes. They had to scramble among themselves to get the best morsel sometimes. And they themselves sometimes became food for a bigger enemy.

But with God, as David learned, all of his needs—spiritual, physical, and emotional—were met. Always. "Oh, the joys of those who take refuge in him!" David sang in this psalm. Even strong, young lions go hungry. But as he declared, "Those who fear [God] will have all they need" (vv. 8-9).

In our spiritual imaginations, we can picture David singing this psalm—composed to celebrate the time he outsmarted Abimelech. Perhaps he recalled his years shepherding sheep and fending off wild animals. So those lions sometimes went away hungry, David remembered. But when we trust in God, His blessing of grace, love, and power provides for all.

The God of the Bible is the kind of God whose greatest delight comes not from making demands but from meeting needs.
SAM STORMS

41

Knowledge of God

❧

Knowledge of the Holy One results in good judgment.
PROVERBS 9:10

Let me teach you.
MATTHEW 11:29

Remember the smartest kid in your class? The real "brain"? The guy or gal everybody envied for his or her book smarts? Maybe that person was you. Or maybe you were the street-smart kid—smart enough to survive on life's mean streets, but not much for books. Both kinds of knowledge have value.

But the best knowledge for life—for making the best decisions throughout life, to navigate the many twists and turns of life and to give the best back to life—is to know the Holy God.

The holiness of God as a subject of study is so life changing, says the writer of this ninth chapter of Proverbs, that it multiplies our days and adds years to our lives.

To know God as holy expands and completes everything else we need to learn for life. As the Holy

One, God is sacred and set apart, above everything and everyone.

But as we expand our thinking about what it means that God is holy, we realize God isn't just sacred and set apart. As holy, God also is whole and complete. Wholesome. Healthy. Hearty. *And* holy.

To know this about God—and to personally know Him as holy—impacts every judgment call and decision we will make in life, big or small, with the hearty and healthy holiness of the God we serve. The blessing?

Good judgment. Not silly judgment. Or stupid or frivolous or immoral or amoral or biased or dumb or ditzy or depressive judgment. Instead, seek to know God as holy. Then watch something remarkable happen to your decision making. In a hearty and healthy, whole and holy way, your judgment will be transformed.

---

*A true love of God must begin with
a delight in his holiness.*
JONATHAN EDWARDS

42

Knowledge of Self

We ask God to give you complete knowledge.
COLOSSIANS 1:9

Know thyself. Since ancient times, philoso-
phers have urged our inner knowledge. But
the Bible encourages us to approach it differently.
"Commune with your own heart upon your bed,"
says Psalm 4:4 (KJV). Take some good time, that is,
to know how God wired you. Then marvel at how
He made you and use His unique creation to glorify
and bless Him. Complete knowledge of ourselves,
yes, glorifies Him.

A lot of work, in fact—this knowing ourselves.

But when it comes to looking inward completely,
what exactly should we know?

First, know your gifts. Your strengths. That
special anointing placed in each of us by God's
Spirit. "Each person has a special gift from God"
(1 Corinthians 7:7). What's yours? Can't figure it
out? Ask God to show you. Then as you seek God
for this self-awareness and discover it, you'll see how
to best give back to God's Kingdom. Even if it looks

unusual. In fact, the more unusual it looks, the more correct it probably is.

So also know your weaknesses. Your temptations. Your shortcomings. And what evangelist Arthur Pink calls our "constitutional sins"—that "particular turn or cast of mind" by which we are most in danger of sinning against God and our neighbor. Examine it thoroughly, Pink says. "Every man has his weak side, and every wise man knows where it is, and will be sure to keep a double guard there."

At the same time, know your needs—those things that matter most to you—so you can explain yourself to others close to you. We can't read minds. So know your priorities, then bless others by telling them—so they can address those needs if possible.

Most important, know who you are in Christ. Victorious. Triumphant. A new creature in Him. Able to do all things through Christ who strengthens you beyond any weakness because He shines brighter.

And that's not just a slogan. That's the beautiful blessing of complete knowledge of Him.

The man is what his heart is.
ARTHUR PINK

43

Prudence for Life

The prudent understand where they are going.
PROVERBS 14:8

On the road of life, we sometimes get lost. But we don't have to stay lost. We have a guide, and He tells us exactly where we are going—to His glory, being transformed to His likeness (2 Corinthians 3:18). Then He tells us how to get there.

Be prudent.

But I laughed at this word. It sounded prudish and proper. But then I sat down and read. And the joke was on me. Because a prudent person, according to any good dictionary, is a planner—wisely avoiding mistakes or faults—by looking down the road at what's to come. So prudent people aren't "prudes." They're cautious and circumspect, looking at all sides of a situation and, therefore, careful in their conduct.

This deep power in being prudent is seen in its Latin origin, *prudens*, meaning "to foresee." In fact, it's a contraction of the Latin word *providens*, or provident, meaning "to see ahead." Seeing ahead those things that could possibly trip us up or bring us down or that pose a danger, prudent people act accordingly.

Thus, seeing ahead, prudent people plan for retirement.

Thus, seeing ahead, prudent people repair the roof when the sun is shining—instead of waiting until it falls apart in the rain.

Thus, seeing ahead, prudent people seek out strong, honest friends who can lift them up in life—they do not fool around with lazy, dishonest ne'er-do-wells wrangling for a free ride.

"Fools deceive themselves," says Proverbs 14:8. But "the prudent understand where they are going." With eyes wide open, they look down the road of life and plan as God advises. Then they live accordingly, expecting an outcome that God can bless.

Can you see your blessed life? Look down the road today. Ask your loved ones to do the same. Then with understanding, respond together with the visionary blessing and grace of empowered prudence.

God's providence is not blind, but full of eyes.
JOHN GREENLEAF WHITTIER

44

Prudence for Family

A prudent person foresees danger and takes precautions.
PROVERBS 22:3

Nobody likes to think about the worst. Not even Christians. So some believers argue that preparing ahead for emergencies shows a lack of faith. But while we can respect each other's convictions on such matters, we might consider how one notable Bible hero was blessed by looking ahead. Yes, prudently.

I'm talking here of Joseph in the book of Genesis.

Known as an interpreter of dreams, Joseph was saved from a prison cell in Egypt when only he, with God's help, could interpret the pharaoh's dreams. As Joseph explained to Pharaoh, the leader's dream meant that seven years of prosperity in Egypt would be followed by seven years of famine. Famine "so severe that even the memory of the good years will be erased" (Genesis 41:31).

But Joseph wasn't finished. Appoint a good adviser to manage the crisis, saving back food from good years to use during bad years, he counseled Pharaoh.

Impressed with Joseph's foresight, Pharaoh put the ex-prisoner Joseph in charge of all of Egypt. His job included overseeing a national plan to collect, in the fat years, the surplus crops. Then in lean years, enough food would be on hand to save the people.

And sure enough, prosperity came to Egypt for seven years. Followed by seven years of famine. But thanks to prudent Joseph, when famine struck, he "opened up the storehouses and distributed grain to the Egyptians." But that's not all. "People from all around came to Egypt to buy grain" (Genesis 41:56-57). Among them were the brothers who'd betrayed him long before.

In fact, Joseph's prudent planning saved not only Egypt, but also the people of Israel and the lineage of Christ. Prudent planning, for certain. God blesses it.

Still fearful to plan? Stand up and be prudent, like Joseph—looking ahead to God for your long-range provision. Then watch with joy as He beautifully blesses you for the long haul.

The best preparation for tomorrow
is doing your best today.
H. JACKSON BROWN JR.

45

Mercy All My Life

*Surely goodness and mercy shall follow
me all the days of my life.*

PSALM 23:6, KJV

Why David? That's what I wondered. Why such mercy for him? And why such goodness for a man with appalling sins—especially that matter with Bathsheba, including the illicit sex, the murder, the whole disconcerting mess.

And yet. David, of all people in the Bible—and with astonishing certainty—states clearly that goodness and mercy will follow him. Surely. And not just for a little while. Forever.

Brazen confidence? Or knowledge that God's goodness and mercy—His "unfailing love," as the New Living Translation describes it—will pursue those who pursue God? Always it will follow them. What a strong, sweet promise for all of us broken, sinful believers. Like David, we've all fallen short. Big-time. My own sins are as red as scarlet.

But God won't give up on us. On pursuing us. On chasing us down. On running after us, time and again, to pick us up and set us right while He pours His unfailing love into our broken, dirty, bruised—and sometimes stupid—hearts.

It was stupid, for sure, for David to have sex with another man's wife, then arrange for her husband to die in battle. David's twenty-third psalm reminds us, however, that not even a perverted act of adultery—with murder on the side—is too much for God to forgive, then to repair with His sweet mercy.

Do you feel guilty for past wrongs? Then pray like David. But this time, says theologian R. C. Sproul, "don't ask Him to forgive you for the sin that is haunting you. Rather, ask Him to forgive you for insulting His integrity by refusing to accept His forgiveness." His mercy is a gift—and it's in pursuit. Let us stop running today. Then the blessing of mercy will catch us.

Right now counts forever.
R. C. Sproul

46

Mercy in Kind

God blesses those who are merciful,
for they will be shown mercy.

MATTHEW 5:7

William Shakespeare tried to capture the essence of mercy in his tragic comedy *The Merchant of Venice.* "The quality of mercy is not strained," says his character Portia in the play. "It droppeth as the gentle rain from heaven. . . . It blesseth him that gives and him that takes. . . . It is an attribute to God himself."

While various scholars have debated the underlying meanings of Portia's plea to the moneylender Shylock, her "mercy speech" stands out for seeing that mercy blesses going and coming. In fact, in the Beatitudes of Jesus, from which today's Scripture is taken, mercy is the only attribute shown to reproduce itself in kind. That is, those who are merciful "will be shown mercy." Not so with the other Beatitudes—as in blessed are the poor for "the Kingdom of Heaven is given to them." Or blessed are those who mourn for "they will be comforted" (vv. 3, 4).

Mercy, however, as Shakespeare's Portia declares, "is an attribute to God himself." So mercy is a gentle gift, dropping from our spirits as "rain from heaven." Only by God's Holy Spirit, indeed, can any of us not forever hold somebody accountable for a wrong. In kind, that same person can cut us some slack when we fall short.

The nature of humanity is to mess up. Sometimes a lot. Sometimes big-time.

Mercy steps back from human frailty to grant, not a pardon, but godly understanding. So mercy acknowledges wrong. But mercy doesn't force people to stay pinned to the ground in their error. Mercy extends a hand. To lift up. To pull the fallen to their feet. We can do the same today. Just as God does for us. As we do, God promises a blessed payback for mercy. More mercy to us.

Heaven have mercy on us all—Presbyterians and pagans alike—for we are all somehow dreadfully cracked about the head, and sadly need mending.
HERMAN MELVILLE

Mercy Like God

Shouldn't you have mercy on your fellow servant, just as I had mercy on you?

MATTHEW 18:33

After twenty-plus years of marriage, the woman's husband confessed. Along the way in their marriage, he'd had sex with another woman. Or maybe more than one. The full truth was emerging slowly. But this truth—and the debilitating pain it caused these many years later—left her bitter, angry, hungry for revenge.

But as this woman shared the story of this deep trauma to her marriage, she revealed how she coped and how they finally healed. "I had mercy." Rather than rake her repentant husband over the coals with her hurt—then force him to grovel in the full details of the betrayals, again and again—she took her pain to God. She left it there with God. Then she offered her husband what it seemed he didn't deserve. Her mercy.

Just like God offers His mercy to us. Even when we don't deserve it.

Then the miracle. "My own healing," she said. "I could feel the pain start to lift. With ups and downs, yes. But healing nonetheless." Even more, the marriage healed too. More sooner than later, in fact.

She could've taken another path, acting like the unmerciful servant in a parable of Jesus (Matthew 18:21-35). After begging for mercy, the servant was forgiven his big debt—of millions of dollars—by the merciful king. But when a fellow servant, who owed him a few thousand dollars, begged for mercy, the unmerciful servant "grabbed him by the throat and demanded instant payment" (v. 28). Likewise, this woman, whose own sins have been forgiven by God, could've grabbed her husband by the throat and demanded emotional payback, forgetting how God had shown mercy for her flaws. But mercy prevailed. Then healing followed. Are you hurting today from a deep betrayal and driven to pay it back with reprisals? Ask the Holy Spirit to empower you to pay back the hurt with the unthinkable. With His mercy.

Then watch God make a miracle by granting you His healing and mercy too.

There is healing in the telling.
CECIL MURPHEY

48

Self-Control: By His Spirit

*But the Holy Spirit produces this
kind of fruit in our lives.*

GALATIANS 5:22

So now, here comes the hard spiritual fruit.
Self-control.

But self-control isn't gritting our teeth. Instead,
as theologian Richard Foster might say, self-control
is falling in love.

Especially with God's Spirit. Then it's inviting
God's Spirit to dwell in our hearts, minds, souls, and
bodies—each day. Every hour.

I need to think about that today. A day when I
need the blessed assurance that God loves me and
His Spirit longs to dwell in me. So I need to stop
trying so hard to control myself. In fact, when I consider self-control, I might want to stand down and
be quiet. The human idea of self-control, that is, can
seem so hard. Who's *that* perfect? That disciplined?
Great questions, it would seem.

But the Bible helps us find the best answer—that
self-control isn't forcing ourselves not to indulge

in our human lusts. It's not gritting our teeth and screaming, "*I will not* gamble, cheat, smoke, overeat, worship idols, sexually sin, get drunk, act jealous, show envy, fight, do drugs, throw wild parties—or anything else." In fact, self-control doesn't shout at all.

Self-control whispers. *I surrender.* Yes, quiet words. *Come in, Holy Spirit.*

Talk about a great prayer to whisper each day! *Come in.* Then all the fruits of the Spirit—love, joy, peace, patience, kindness, goodness, faithfulness, gentleness, *and* self-control—become evident. Or as Jesus said so beautifully: "You will receive power when the Holy Spirit comes upon you. And you will be my witnesses" (Acts 1:8).

"Supergood" people may act good. But they miss out on the relationship. Self-control is about falling in love. *So come in, Holy Spirit.*

Have you issued that invitation to the Lord? Draw near and whisper those words today. The beautiful fruit of self-control will hear, bless, and follow.

Jesus shows us a more excellent way.
The way of helplessness.
RICHARD FOSTER

49

Self-Control with Strength

*A person without self-control is like a
city with broken-down walls.*
PROVERBS 25:28

Even in young children, self-control pays off.
In a famous experiment from the sixties called
the Marshmallow Test, psychologists at Stanford
University determined that kids who could say no to
eating a marshmallow did better in school and in life.

The kids were just four years old.

Each was given a marshmallow, then promised
another one—but only if they could wait fifteen
minutes before eating the first one. Some children
managed to wait. Others could not. The research
team then followed the progress of each child into
their teen years. What did they find? The children
with greater self-control as four-year-olds tested
higher as teens on key life variables—such as happiness, psychological adjustment, and dependability.
They also scored significantly higher on the SAT.

To lack self-control is to end up just as the Bible
predicts. We're left weak and vulnerable, with holes

in our armor and weak spots in our defenses—"like a city with broken-down walls." But there's good news. We can improve our self-control—building up and strengthening our life's walls. How?

Make self-denial a lifestyle. Trying to lose weight? Take a nutrition class to learn how to eat right. Trying to cut down on your computer time? Plan time instead to help others or to learn a new skill. Struggling to stop smoking? Don't go it alone. Join others in a stop-smoking program.

Then practice self-control as a lifestyle. Dirty dishes in the sink? Wash them. Piles of clothes on the stairs? Pick them up. Missing a button on a blouse? Sew it on. Soon you'll see how your attention to one area positively influences your actions in all areas. Remind yourself today that self-control matters to God. He wants His children to enjoy strong lives—not broken down by weakness. So on this day, invite His Spirit in to bless and empower this journey. With every step, you'll find more strength. Not yours. His.

When you surrender your will to God, you discover the resources to do what God requires.
Erwin Lutzer

50

Contentment with Godliness

True godliness with contentment is itself great wealth.
1 TIMOTHY 6:6

They were church people in Ephesus, but they craved great wealth. Grasped for it. Schemed for it. Then they took the lowest of the low roads to obtain their wealth. They taught that God would give rich people even more wealth—a prosperity gospel of some sort—if they'd pay up yet more money to the church. Then they'd all be rolling in dough—all enjoying fat-cat cash.

A lie. That's what the apostle Paul warns Timothy about this scheme.

"These people always cause trouble. Their minds are corrupt, and they have turned their backs on the truth" (v. 5).

Wealth to them, that is, was all about money—and their hopes of feeding some deep spiritual discontentment with the false satisfaction of money.

Great wealth, however, is about godly well-being, Paul writes.

It's a teaching that should sink deep daily into

every believer's heart. As it does, we understand, as Paul says, that "if we have enough food and clothing" (v. 8), we can be content. So instead of pursuing monetary wealth—a path that traps people with temptations and "many foolish and harmful desires" (v. 9)—let's reach for godly wealth.

Indeed, "pursue righteousness," Paul writes, "and a godly life, along with faith, love, perseverance, and gentleness" (v. 11). In these simple and beautiful things we find spiritual wealth, yes—in fact, *great* spiritual wealth.

No denying, surely, that monetary wealth can buy pretty things. But great wealth buys "the eternal life to which God has called you" (v. 12), Paul writes. So don't spend your life pursuing earthly wealth, which in the end can stir up foolish desires, plunging us "into ruin and destruction" (v. 9), Paul warns. Instead ask God today to replace your craving for "wealth" with a craving for *great* wealth. The beautiful contentment that results will bless you now—but even better, it will bless you forever.

Contentment comes from trusting God.
JOHN MACARTHUR

51

Contentment: For God

*Then others began coming—men who were in
trouble or in debt or who were just discontented—
until David was the captain of about 400 men.*

1 SAMUEL 22:2

Is all discontent bad? Not always. That's important
to know. In church, when we talk about contentment, we often act like discontent can be only bad.

Good discontent, however, provides the perfect
warning. It says something deep in our lives is
wrong, wrong, wrong. That the only right thing—
and the only way to find that right thing—is to
come to God.

The psalmist of Psalm 42 captures that feeling
perfectly: "As the deer longs for streams of water, so I
long for you, O God. I thirst for God, the living God.
When can I go and stand before him?" (vv. 1-2).

Thirst. Longing. This is the cry of someone who
has tried everything, been everywhere, bought everything, been everything. But now discontent—a holy
discontent—finally cries out for the only One who
can give lasting satisfaction.

As you read about contentment today, are you *dis*contented? With yourself? Your career? Your spouse? Your kids? Your home? Your finances? Your lot in life? Pay attention to this longing and point it to God. Then as you pray, acknowledge your discontent.

That's what the men in the twenty-second chapter of 1 Samuel did. Many were in debt, in trouble—worn down, wrung out, and just flat-out disheartened. They came to David, forming an army of some four hundred. Scholars of the Bible say this incident foreshadows Jesus, who would attract to Himself the down-and-out, the hurting, the outcast, the lost, the burdened—then transform them into His army, the body of Christ. Sound like you?

Are you discontented today? In a good way? Praise God for His holy signal that He's calling you. Run to Him, discontent and all. As you sink into His presence, rejoice that you've taken your thirst and hunger to the right place. Then rest. The blessing of godly contentment is at hand.

Contentment comes only from God, and the sooner we start seeking it in Him, the better off we will be.
RICHARD D. AND SHARON L. PHILLIPS

52

Contentment with Others

If one part is honored, all the parts are glad.
1 CORINTHIANS 12:26

Somebody else always has more. Not just in things. But in spiritual gifts, too. In our churches, therefore, when different people have vastly different gifts—and some appear to be more spiritually gifted than others—the ugly green monster called jealousy can rear its discontented head. Just like in the world.

In the church, however, such discontent can leave us deceived and disheartened. For in comparing ourselves with others, we'll find ourselves overestimating somebody else's talents—or underestimating our own.

As Paul tells the Christians in Galatia, "Pay careful attention to your own work, for then you will get the satisfaction of a job well done, and you won't need to compare yourself to anyone else. For we are each responsible for our own conduct" (Galatians 6:4-5).

In short, we all have gifts. It doesn't matter, therefore, if somebody else's gift appears more important. Or if they get more attention. Or more credit. Or if they use their gifts in big or small ways. In fact, judging others for how they use their gifts is not our business. So here's a reminder for us all.

Love each other—and each other's gifts. Then *relax*.

In our churches, says Paul, there will be apostles, prophets, teachers, healers, and more—all with our quirks, hiccups, complexities, and kooky, sometimes maddening ways. But if we appreciate each other's gifts, then lay down, as theologian Richard Foster says, "the everlasting burden of always needing to manage others," we'll be blessed with contentment. But not just with others. We'll be content with ourselves.

Is that your challenge today? Find somebody in your church who's hard for you to love—because his or her gift seems greater. Then love that person anyway. You'll be overjoyed at how much, in turn, you love God and yourself.

Love the body of Christ—our true brothers and sisters—in such a way that the world and spiritual powers are stunned by our oneness.
EDWARD T. WELCH

53

Dignity and Modesty: In Behavior

When you bow down before the Lord and admit your dependence on him, he will lift you up and give you honor.

JAMES 4:10

Thousands watched in the rain while the pop singer—"the most popular living person on Facebook"—belted out songs at an outdoor concert. To fuel the public's fixation with her celebrity persona, she wore look-at-me outfits—gyrating provocatively in front of a chorus line of equally provocative backup dancers.

Still I didn't watch. Turning the channel, I thought about what psychologists say about the public's fascination with celebrities, celebrity fashions, and celebrity behavior. "Celebrities are fascinating because they live in a parallel universe—one that looks and feels just like ours yet is light-years beyond our reach." So says Carlin Flora, features editor at *Psychology Today* magazine. Compared to our dull and safe lives, their lives seem exciting, important, and enviable. That's what we tell ourselves, anyway. "Stars summon our most human yearnings: to love, admire, copy and, of course, to gossip and to jeer," Flora adds.

Then comes James. The brother of Jesus reminds us of the dangers of worshiping the brazen immodesty of pop-culture icons. "Don't you realize that friendship with this world makes you an enemy of God?" (v. 4).

Does that mean God hates pop singers and Hollywood celebrities? I feel certain He does not. In fact, I'd argue God loves these pop icons as much as He loves the least celebrated among us. He sent His Son to die for us all.

But when we return His love by fawning over the immodesty and indignity of certain cultural idols, we cozy up to the devil—pushing God away. Our gossip on Facebook about stars and their coarse displays can feel fun. But stop laughing, says James. Instead "let there be sorrow and deep grief. Let there be sadness instead of laughter, and gloom instead of joy" (v. 9). Turn from false fun. Instead, uplift the beauty of wholesome. Then bow down before the Lord, showing your dependence on Him. As you bow, He will lift you up—blessing you with honor. Not like a pop star. But like His own Son.

Remember that God's approval is infinitely
more important than the world's.
BRUCE BARTON

54

Silence and Solitude: To Hear God's Voice

After the fire there was the sound of a gentle whisper.

· 1 KINGS 19:12

The wall-to-wall sound system was a monster. And my husband was in love. "*Wow*." He stood in the appliance store, awestruck, facing the fancy amplifiers as they pounded out a movie sound track. "Can you *feel* that?" He was mesmerized.

I nodded, smiling, impressed but secretly praying: *Please, don't let him buy that!*

Of course, to hear sound is a blessed gift. I understand that. But later, I thought about the sound of God.

The prophet Elijah hears this sound only by God's mercy. In fact, God is chastising Elijah for running away in fear from the evil and godless Queen Jezebel—and hiding in a cave. "What are you doing here, Elijah?" (v. 9).

It's a question most of us have heard. Heard in our hearts.

As we've stood in the storms, earthquakes, and fires in our lives, then tried to run, weren't we surprised to learn that God didn't speak in upheavals? Yet *after* them, when we finally stopped swirling and worrying and shaking in our boots, the gentle stillness of God—always there—could finally be heard.

So it is with Elijah. Humbled and duly aware of the quiet whisper of God's power, he yanks off his cloak and wraps it around his face—his reverence raw and awestruck. Can you *feel* that? He might, as my husband in the appliance store, want to ask such a question about the sound of God. It is so intense yet so soft. Yet we won't hear or feel it if we don't quiet our storms and seek His face. Not running from God, but running to Him.

God's still voice? To hear it, turn off the loud sounds of life. Open His Word and listen. Unlock your spirit and hear. Turn from your storms, your fires, your earthquakes. And feel. What will you hear? The empowered blessing of His answer.

Listen to the inward Voice 'til you learn to recognize it.
A. W. Tozer

55

Silence and Solitude: In Worship to God

*Be silent before the LORD, all humanity,
for he is springing into action.*
ZECHARIAH 2:13

O Lord, my God. Did A. W. Tozer, the self-taught theologian, pray like this? I suspect he did. A word or two. Then silence. Or as Tozer put it: "Retire from the world each day to some private spot, even if it be only the bedroom." Or for Tozer, the furnace room "for want of a better place."

Now that's a provocative picture. Imagine Tozer, one of the most well-loved Bible teachers and speakers of his time, alone in the basement with himself and with his God next to the furnace. Or perhaps that makes perfect sense. In that humble place, this man Tozer—who spoke before crowds of hundreds and thousands—would've felt his real humanity. There, in the steam heat of winter and the cold darkness of summer, he would best understand: When we worship God in our own still silence, we finally hear. That God *isn't* silent. In fact, God is springing into action.

Like Tozer, the prophet Zechariah in today's Scripture understood that. Worshiping God in silence, the prophet was able to hear this message: Don't stay trapped in exile or captivity—whatever your personal Babylon might be.

"The LORD says, 'Shout and rejoice, O beautiful Jerusalem, for I am coming to live among you. . . . I will live among you, and you will know that the LORD of Heaven's Armies sent me to you" (vv. 10-11).

What blessed assurance—to be reminded that Jesus our Christ is already moving on our circumstances, springing into action, even before we speak a word about it. Our tendency is to bend God's ears with our worries, thereby staying trapped with them—in a Babylon of our own making. But both Zechariah and the self-taught preacher Tozer urge us to consider silence. As we quiet our panic, God springs into action for those who dare, in silence, to believe.

Stay in the secret place till the surrounding noises begin to fade out of your heart and a sense of God's presence envelops you.
A. W. TOZER

56

Silence and Solitude: To Gain God's Perspective

It is good to wait quietly.
LAMENTATIONS 3:26

What's the best way to open our minds? Close our mouths.

Dare I try it? Or will I have to learn like Zechariah, the husband of Elizabeth?

I study his story with close attention. If you recall it, Zechariah in old age was told he and his aged and barren wife would have a son. This child would become John the Baptist. But Zechariah doubted. He asked God's messenger Gabriel for proof. "How can I know this will happen?" (Luke 1:18).

Wrong question. It lacked faith.

Therefore, said Gabriel, "since you didn't believe what I said, you won't be able to speak until the child is born" (v. 20). Nine months of silence. Lots of time to think. Silent time. In fact, when the child finally was born and Elizabeth said his name would be John—a name never before used in their family's priestly line—Zechariah finally understood God's plan. The child would be John the Baptist, indeed. Asking for a writing tablet, Zechariah scratched out: "His name is John!" (v. 63).

Instantly, Zechariah could speak again.

"And he began praising God" (v. 64).

Few of us would want to gain godly perspective from such an imposed silence. The story, however, illustrates how purposeful silence can open our minds to God. The prophet Jeremiah made this same case in the book of Lamentations. During the darkest period of his life, he came to understand that, as bad as things were, God's mercy saved him from even worse. "It is good to wait quietly for salvation from the LORD."

Is this a perspective you can use today? Not just that holy silence yields fresh understanding—but that God is faithful through all of it. His love is unfailing, resulting in salvation and deliverance. Now that's understanding worth waiting for. How can you and I test it today? Silently.

God speaks in the silence of the heart.
MOTHER TERESA

57

The Sacrifice of Our Prayers

Ask me.

JEREMIAH 33:3

God is waiting. He wants to hear from us today. To hear from me. To hear from you. To connect up in that amazing communion between mortality and immortality—whereby the Sovereign Power of the universe hears our personal, private requests— then answers.

Yet daily prayer, unlike five other faith habits, has not seen an increase among those who practice it, according to experts. In a study, The Barna Group examined seven religious faith habits—including Bible reading, church attendance, church volun- teerism, and Sunday school attendance. While prayer is the most practiced faith behavior, the percentage of respondents who say they pray daily has not changed since 1993. The only other behavior that showed no increased practice by believers? Evangelizing, or telling someone about Jesus. We get cold feet, appar- ently, when it comes to sharing Christ.

But, first, back to prayer.

We know it blesses us. We know it blesses God. In fact, we know God desires our prayers—and that, indeed, He rewards those who diligently seek Him.

"Ask me," He told the prophet Jeremiah, "and I will tell you some remarkable secrets about what is going to happen here." But should God have had to plead with Jeremiah to stop long enough to commune with Him? Should He have to plead with us?

Have we forgotten that prayer is how God works in His world? That, as the psalmist was told by God, "When they call on me, I will answer" (Psalm 91:15).

To be sure, when Jesus arose very early in the morning—"long before daybreak"—and went alone into the wilderness to pray (Mark 1:35), He *always* returned with fresh answers. With renewed energy. With a revived spirit. To be certain, He returned with power. Then why not you? Will you sacrifice prayer to God? Right now? He is waiting for your offering. Mine, too. Let us bless Him by sacrificing our praises and our requests, then watch with wonder as He blesses us with love—empowering us to tell others He lives.

> *God expects to hear from you, before you*
> *can expect to hear from Him.*
> WILLIAM GURNALL

58

The Sacrifice of Our Broken Hearts

⌒∽⌒

The sacrifice you desire is a broken spirit. You will not reject a broken and repentant heart, O God.

PSALM 51:17

King David couldn't believe he'd done wrong. His sin had so poisoned his spirit that he couldn't see the audacity and horror of all he'd dared to do.

But when his adviser confronted him—looked him in the eye and challenged him for adultery and murder, for duplicity and deception—then David could see. *He had sinned.* Sinned against God. "Against you, and you alone, have I sinned," he confessed to God. "I have done what is evil in your sight" (v. 4).

So no ritual sacrifice would be enough to atone.

No burnt offering. No extra tithe. No volunteering to paint the church kitchen or to take food to the poor or to plant some flowers around the church parking lot.

Those are all good things. To do good and share with those in need pleases God.

When we sin, however, God wants our hearts. Broken.

Only then can He rebuild our lives—start the work of putting us back together again in His way. It's quite beautiful to see, in fact, as David finally saw, that a broken spirit excites God.

It shows we trust Him to do what we can't do ourselves—make ourselves right.

So I dare today to think, not about my sins, but about my heart.

I imagine it broken. Gathered up in a simple cardboard box.

It's not fancy enough to offer to God. Yet I can imagine Him reaching down to receive it.

He accepts it. It's a treasure to God. A priceless gift to God. Thus, with love, He takes a cracked and bruised piece. Holds it. Loves it. Mends it. Heals it. Your heart, too. He is taking it up and renewing— not rejecting—this sacrifice of a broken heart. True, we have sinned. But He redeems. The place to start? In the beautiful blessing of our broken hearts.

What is the first thing we need, in order to be Christians? A new heart.
J. C. RYLE

59

Resting in His Invitation

*Come to me, all of you who are weary and carry
heavy burdens, and I will give you rest.*

MATTHEW 11:28

She couldn't sleep. Bone tired. But she couldn't
rest. "Family trouble," this woman explained.
Her mental turmoil, that is, was taking a big toll on
her body. Feeling worn-out and stressed, her mind
racing with anxiety, she couldn't calm herself enough
to sleep right or rest well.

That's perhaps how Jesus' new followers were
feeling.

Torn between their old beliefs, with heavy legal
requirements set by the Pharisees and religious
leaders—and a new life and family in Christ—they
were worn out with worried stress. But Jesus offered
spiritual refreshment.

"Come to me," He invited them. "All of you."

He issues the same invitation to us today. Yes, to
all of us.

Come.

It's the perfect invitation. An offer from Jesus

Himself. He alone knows how spiritual turmoil feels, and He alone can do something about it.

We are weary, and He knows. We are burdened, and He knows. We are carrying more worry than any of us should try to carry, thinking foolishly that carrying around our emotional or spiritual burdens— like martyrs—will somehow enable us to fix them.

Knowing better, Jesus offers not an answer to our problems—but an invitation to simply leave them with Him, then to rest *while He works them out*.

Rest equals trust, that is. We rest in Christ, not because He offers His rest, but because He delivers on the invitation. His invitation still stands today.

Come to Me and rest. We'll hear no better words today or ever. Stand up and bless Him with your yes. Then sit down. He wants to bless you with rest.

God is calling us from others to him.
DALE HANSON BOURKE

60

Resting in His Sufficiency

*Let my soul be at rest again, for the
LORD has been good to me.*

PSALM 116:7

Jesus is enough. So stop striving.

Afraid to stop? Ditch the fear and stop striving, even if you're scared. In today's Scripture, the psalmist is pausing to remind himself of exactly that. Sure, he could panic. Then he remembers:

How kind the Lord is! How good He is! Or as he adds: "I was facing death, and he saved me" (v. 6). *So let my soul be at rest.* Again.

What's his point? That the well of God never runs dry. It refreshes us, again and again. And that's as it should be. A onetime rest with God, just like a once-a-year vacation, isn't enough.

Instead, we go back to the Lord—over and over—for yet more of His rest. He is, as He Himself declared, Lord of the Sabbath. In Him, we can cease from our own work, and struggling over our own work, we can rest in His.

Don't you need that?

I do. I've worked hard so far this year, as I'm sure you have.

I've thrown back my feeble shoulders, toiled and labored, struggled and strained, aiming to give my best to the Lord. Or trying to. But all my labor is in vain if I don't trust the Lord to transform the least of my human efforts into His divine all.

So on this day, Jesus, let me know it's okay to take a break every now and then from this toiling. But especially, remind me that You are good.

That's enough for all of us to know today. And to rest in today.

Then, sweet Jesus, as we rejoice in Your goodness, and in Your sufficiency, we're reminded to put down our plans and tools, turn off our devices, lie in the sunshine, and indulge ourselves in the complete and wondrous All-ness of You.

God is both the water and the hose,
the Supply and the Supplier.
KIRBYJON CALDWELL

61

Resting in His Love

God gives rest to his loved ones.

PSALM 127:2

Life isn't a competition. It doesn't have to be, that is. But yours still is?

Then why not drop out of your rat race? Indeed, the race to win and always be on top is the wrong long-distance battle if ever there was one. We want others to like us, to admire us. But also we want God to love us.

Many of us still think we must do a lot to convince Him to grant His love.

But it's the opposite. King Solomon explains:

"It is useless for you to work so hard from early morning until late at night, anxiously working for food to eat." Why? "For God gives rest to his loved ones" (v. 2).

But will we accept that gift?

Will we own less, and have less to take care of? Will we eat less, and have fewer things to buy and cook? Will we worry less? Trust more? Stop comparing other people's blessings with ours? Even if they seem to have more? And if not envying feels hard?

A restful life is noncompetitive, indeed, because it's a trusting life. We believe what we're doing for God is pleasing to Him and what He gives to us is enough.

But how to arrive at such trust? Let's take a cue from Lynne Baab, author of *Sabbath Keeping: Finding Freedom in the Rhythms of Rest.* In it, she describes how she and her husband, while living in Israel, learned to accept God's rest because, from sunset Friday to sunset Saturday, everything around them was closed. Buses didn't run. Theaters, stores, and restaurants closed. So they read books. Walked. Talked. Her husband went bird-watching. Or they napped. Prayed together. Describing the practice to TodaysChristianWoman.com, she explains: "We rested in God's love and experienced his grace." Away from the rat race.

But here's the great secret about such rest. If we learn not to strive on Sunday, we learn to live in God's rest every day. We work hard and well. But without envy, doubt, or competing. Then we rest. It's a gift. Let's start now and open it.

Help me, Lord, to work resting and to pray resting.
RICHARD FOSTER

62

Justice That's Holy and That Heals

The LORD is close to the brokenhearted;
he rescues those whose spirits are crushed.

PSALM 34:18

You were wronged. Maybe by a friend. A family member. A wife. A husband. A coworker. A boss. By life itself.

If so, you're in good company. Who among us hasn't been hurt deeply, sometimes by people we love—but sometimes by complete strangers? Or sometimes by the vagaries and whims of life. No matter how our hurt happened, however, hurt still hurts. Pain is still pain. To be betrayed, misused, defamed, wrongly accused, lied about, or harmed in any way—emotionally or physically—leaves us reeling. Ready for revenge. Ready to aim and fire and blast to smithereens the one who did us wrong.

But we must not be deceived. Revenge is not our work. We can't judge our hurts right. We're sinners too. And God knows this. So He specifically cautioned against avenging our own pain. He'll handle it Himself. Perfectly just, His justice is perfect.

"I will take revenge; I will pay them back," He says in Deuteronomy 32:35. "In due time their feet will slip. Their day of disaster will arrive, and their destiny will overtake them."

God talks tough here. It's tough talk, indeed, to a generation of Israelites who defied and disobeyed Him. But to today's Christians, the apostle Paul lifts the exact same promise in his letter called Romans. "Never pay back evil with more evil. . . . Never take revenge. Leave that to the righteous anger of God. For the Scriptures say, *'I will take revenge; I will pay them back,'* *says the LORD*'" (Romans 12:17, 19, italics added).

But you're still hurting? If so, start trusting.

Trust that if you release your hurt to God—in effect, forgiving the wrongdoer—God will handle the injustice of it. Then comes the bonus. He rescues those broken, crushed wounds in your spirit, making you whole again. That's justice done right. That's justice done holy. Bless God today and trust Him enough to let it happen.

The place of justice is a hallowed place.
FRANCIS BACON

63

Justice That Builds God's Community

Then the LORD your God will bless you in all you do.

DEUTERONOMY 24:19

The children of Israel knew exactly what kind of justice God wanted. They also knew why—to remind them as onetime slaves of Egypt that God had enacted justice for them. As Moses exhorted them, "The LORD your God redeemed you from your slavery. That is why I have given you this command" (v. 18)—to do justice.

Indeed, honor justice for the poor and foreigners. *Then I will bless all you do.*

A commandment with a blessing. So how could they forget?

Yet they did. We all forget, in fact. God's commandments to do right and seek justice seem, somehow, to just slip our minds. Or we get busy. Or other people's problems with poverty and injustice seem like just another segment on the nightly news. Or, to be honest, we don't care too much. We've got better things to do. Like making ourselves comfortable, not to mention making ourselves rich.

That's what happened with the Israelites. Their upper-crust wives oppressed the poor and crushed the needy. Although peasants lived in mud brick, these women begged their dishonest husbands to build them fancy houses of cut stone. Lounging in luxury, their judges took bribes, depriving the poor of justice, trampling the poor through taxes and unfair rents. Then to add insult to injury, they made a big show of worshiping God.

But enough of your religious festivals and "solemn" prayer meetings, God said (Amos 5:21).

Instead, God sought from them true justice— "a mighty flood of justice, an endless river of righteous living" (v. 24).

God, whose justice is "like the ocean depths," David said in Psalm 36:6, now demands a river. Not a trickle. God wants justice to flow. Endlessly. *Give justice to the least.* If we do, His blessings will pour back down to us. Then all of us get renewed, together. That's what a flow of justice creates— community. Many parts, one body. Sealed together with justice and love. So let's bless Him today by blessing the least, all for Him.

Charity begins at home, and justice begins next door.
CHARLES DICKENS

Justice That Protects the Innocent

You must not deny justice to the poor.
EXODUS 23:6

Charles Chatman spent twenty-seven years in a state prison for a 1981 rape he didn't commit. With DNA evidence, and the help of the Dallas district attorney's office and the nonprofit Innocence Project, his conviction was overturned in 2008.

But despite entering prison at age twenty and leaving at age forty-seven—and never backing down on his claim that he was innocent—he vowed to put prison behind him. How? By helping others. As he told the Associated Press, "I believe that there are hundreds, and I know of two or three personally, that very well could be sitting in this seat if they had the support and they had the backing that I have."

In fact, if just one percent of America's inmates were innocent—and studies suggest the percentage "may be much higher," says the Innocence Project—that means at least twenty thousand men and women may be serving time for crimes they didn't commit.

But twenty-seven years locked in prison? Chatman, whose original conviction called for ninety-nine years in prison, faced essentially a life sentence. But do we care? Isn't that, indeed, the core issue of injustice for God's people?

I ask the question with mixed emotions. While it's easy to point the finger at injustice occurring in countries halfway around the globe, to look at injustice in our own backyard takes a strong stomach.

But God says look. "He is the great God, the mighty and awesome God," says Moses, "who shows no partiality and cannot be bribed. He ensures that orphans and widows receive justice. He shows love to the foreigners living among you and gives them food and clothing. So you, too, must show love" (Deuteronomy 10:17-19).

And then? "If you obey, you will enjoy a long life in the land" (11:9). But so will others. Then let us bless the least by standing up to act in love.

The administration of justice is the firmest pillar of government.
GEORGE WASHINGTON

65

The Truth of Whom Christ Saves

And now you Gentiles have also heard the truth. . . . And when you believed in Christ, he identified you as his own.

EPHESIANS 1:13

M y cousin was on the phone. *My cousin?* Days ago, I didn't even know he existed. But after talking to kin, exchanging photos, double-checking genealogy, trading e-mails, and finally chatting for one revealing hour, I hung up knowing the truth. This was my cousin—second cousin, actually. But through him, I'd uncovered a link to scores of other long-lost relations.

To dig this far into family roots, however, I also dug up long-buried truth. So a few skeletons came tumbling out. But there is no denying. We are family. And I'm ecstatic. What a precious connection.

It matters more to me, however, to belong to Christ.

Me—a little girl from two hardworking and humble parents—yes, even me. I am deemed worthy enough to be known by Christ. You are too.

Before, only Jewish people should have had this privilege. Important Jews at that.

But now you Gentiles, writes the apostle Paul, "have also heard the truth, the Good News that God saves you. And when you believed in Christ, he identified you as his own" (v. 13).

And look at how He made us official family members: "By giving you the Holy Spirit, whom he promised long ago" (v. 13). In a world where some people don't even know their neighbors, God saw our trust in Him and gave us His greatest gift, His own Spirit.

As Christ's family members, that is, we are His. And that's gospel truth.

So let that truth sink root-deep into your soul. We're members of God's family circle, grafted deep into His spiritual tree—where He'll always keep, protect, provide, and love us. Still not feeling too special today? Give Him every doubt you may still harbor about your worth—yes, every lie you've ever believed about what you haven't yet become. Celebrate instead Whose you are. The truth of His ownership makes you matter. How long? Forever.

His is not a creed, a mere doctrine,
but it is He Himself we have.
Dwight L. Moody

66

Truth That Uses God's Power

*Carefully guard the precious truth
that has been entrusted to you.*

2 Timothy 1:14

My tongue has a life of its own. Not glib, I stumble through conversations. Not witty, I aim for humor and fall flat. Still, I ponder the Scriptures and their warnings about the tongue—that it's "a flame of fire . . . full of wickedness that can ruin your whole life . . . an uncontrollable evil, full of deadly poison" (James 3:6, 8). Hot and cold. Sharp and weak. My tongue can be all of these things.

Until I tell the truth. There's something about putting away pretense, not trying to impress, and just telling it like it is—my own truth, God's own truth—that sets my tongue free.

So, on this day, I step to the microphone.

I'm giving a talk at a church program. Me— the awkward one at parties and social settings. I face a room full of people, who are waiting for me to speak. So I follow Paul's reminder in his letter to Timothy: "Carefully guard the precious truth."

How? "Through the power of the Holy Spirit who lives within us" (2 Timothy 1:14).

Ah, yes. That's how I'll give this talk. Just tell the truth. Then I give my tongue over to God.

It's how we say what needs to be said, but say it in love. It's how we dig down to the truth of our stories, and of God's story, so we can share it in ways that heal and make us and others whole. It's how we "carefully guard the precious truth that has been entrusted" to us. Not by our own power. Or by our own clever words. Or by our own wit or wisdom. Or by biting our tongues to control our mouths.

Instead, we let go and speak truth.

The power of the Holy Spirit who lives within us gives us the right words, making us clear. Confident. Generous. Kind. The Lord's power is never pushy. We just have to open our hearts. Then when we open our mouths, even before a microphone, His truth speaks.

Truth is proper and beautiful at all times and in all places.

FREDERICK DOUGLASS

67

Honesty and Integrity in Our Work Lives

People with integrity walk safely.
PROVERBS 10:9

The children of Israel were waiting at Mount Sinai.
Next stop?

The Promised Land.

But they needed instruction, especially about walking and living with a holy God, and also with each other.

The family life of Israel depended on it. That meant rules. So God's rules, from what the Israelites ate to how they worshiped to how they did business, were recorded by Moses in what we call the book of Leviticus. Even a merchant could find rules in this book.

"Do not use dishonest standards when measuring length, weight, or volume" (Leviticus 19:35).

Crooked merchants hurt the entire community with their dishonesty. Their scales were too heavy on one side and too light on the other. Sneaky, they finagled more loot that way. In the end, however, their dishonesty weakened the nation.

But "people with integrity walk safely."

We all have to walk, for certain. It's the only way to move forward. To reach the next destination, and to travel to our dreams, goals, and hopes, we have to strike out on the path of life.

Then oops! Obstacles wait to trip us up. Tough decisions must be made. Partners must be identified. Strategies must be planned. In life, as well, there is land to buy. Inventory to stockpile. Houses to be bought. Crops to be planted.

Cheat while walking over these challenges and you are certain to fall. The Bible promises it. But deal honestly, our same Bible declares, and you walk in safety. Let's trust that today. Start it at home, of course. But at work, stay honest. In all things today, stay honest. The walk back home will be divinely easy.

Honesty has a beautiful and
refreshing simplicity about it.
CHUCK SWINDOLL

68

Honesty and Integrity in Our Money Matters

*Better to be poor and honest than
to be dishonest and rich.*

PROVERBS 28:6

Better to be poor? Not many would believe that.
Poor, as we see it, isn't the goal we seek. Poor?
We know too well what it means: Lacking. Inferior.
Inadequate. Inefficient.

The words for poor in a dictionary go from bad
. . . *undernourished* . . . *pitiable* . . . to worse . . . *trivial*.

Not one thing about being poor, some might say,
bodes for the good. Such a point is up for debate.
But add *honest* to poor? Then everything changes.

Honest poor people are joyful. They walk safely
through life, kept and protected by God. So the
honest have peace. By living right—and with a
clear conscience—the honest poor sleep at night.
Snoozing like babies. Trustworthy and true, the
honest poor are respected and well liked. Delightful,
in fact, in God's eyes.

As delightful as an eleven-year-old North Carolina
Boy Scout who found and returned a stolen purse

with nearly two thousand dollars inside, then gave forty dollars of his one hundred dollars reward money to his mom. As delightful as the Florida girl who returned a wallet to an out-of-work handyman, deciding the money inside wasn't hers but should go to its rightful owner. Liking how this is sounding?

That's because this rich-poor dichotomy isn't, in fact, about riches or poverty. Instead, in the scenario from the book of Proverbs, the big spotlight shines on honesty. That's what counts most here. Sure, poverty can grind—and wealth enrich.

On either side of the coin, however, honesty is the benchmark.

Should we not aspire then to wealth? Not the point.

Aspire to trust God. With our honesty, then, we show we believe He will provide enough—"pressed down, shaken together to make room for more, running over, and poured into your lap," as Luke 6:38 declares.

So bless God with honesty today, especially in money matters, but in all. God will bless you back with every good gift from above. A generous blessing? Actually, more. God's blessing for honesty is priceless.

Honesty is the best policy.
BENJAMIN FRANKLIN

69

Repentance to Gain a New Walk

The pain caused you to repent and change your ways.

2 CORINTHIANS 7:9

Broken. Oh, I don't want to go there. To bear the breakage. To feel the pain of dropping my heart to the ground. To see the truth of real repentance—that before we turn back to God, we have to throw our hearts to the floor, falling on our faces, spilling out our truth before our God.

With guilt and grief, we collapse before God—acknowledging our sin, our offense, and how it sorrows God. Dishonors God. Misrepresents God. Then, broken with guilt and sorrowful with grief, we offer Him a heart bent to the pavement.

In mud. On dirt. Through burning sand.

Why else would the words *repentance* and *reptile* share the same root?

On the ground, our sinful hearts crawl back to God. A painful trip.

But don't neglect to take it today. Run today, in fact, not first to blessing—but to brokenness. For courage to see sin. For a longing to be rid of it.

"Bend *down* to listen," David cries out in Psalm 102:2 (italics added). "Lean *down* and listen," Daniel cries also in Daniel 9:18 (italics added), and we all understand. This road of repentance starts low. But humbling and painful as it is, this path comes with extraordinary blessings. Our painful turning lets God lift, purge, save, sanctify, heal, empower, and change us too.

That's what the apostle Paul observed in the church at Corinth. His piercing letter of 1 Corinthians so convicted wrongdoers that, after repenting before God, they changed. At first, Paul wrote he was sorry for "that severe letter" (2 Corinthians 7:8) to a sinning church. It hurt. But it hit home. Thus, he rejoiced that he sent it, "not because it hurt you, but because the pain caused you to repent and change your ways" (v. 9).

The pain of sin? The pain of truth about sin? Brutal, indeed.

But don't fear such truth. Instead, fall to the ground and crawl. It's there that God's gentle hand points us to a new way. Then He lifts us, standing, graceful, grateful, blessed, returned to Him. By His Spirit, changed.

A heart is never at the best till it be broken.
RICHARD BAKER

70

Repentance to Gain Holy Joy

You have broken me—now let me rejoice.
PSALM 51:8

David's sin with Bathsheba was down and dirty. We know that. But we keep studying it, wondering about it—amazed at it—asking ourselves, in our Bible study meetings and Sunday school classes, *how could he?*

But he did. Adultery, murder, lying, denial—the whole nine yards.

Just as we've fallen short, David surely fell low.

So his cry to God sounds so much like our own:

Have mercy on me, O God (v. 1). Wash me. Purify me.

Have you cried to God like that? Saying like David: "For I recognize my rebellion; it haunts me day and night" (v. 3). We understand that exactly. Down and dirty sin *is* haunting.

But what if we're not yet haunted? Not yet repentant? Most of us, in fact, probably haven't committed adultery *and* murder—surely not in one sweep.

So it's easy not to be haunted by our sin. Not to

see that our sins, especially sins of omission—the justice we didn't seek, the mercy we didn't give, the humility we didn't walk in—break God's heart.

Yet we want joy? In fact, we can have it. But first?

Fall down. Drop to our faces, like David, understanding—like David—that God doesn't want our sacrifices or our worthless burnt offerings. God wants broken spirits.

"You will not reject a broken and repentant heart, O God" (v. 17).

So here is mine.

Break it, precious Christ. Then put back the pieces—scar tissue and all—in a pattern that shows Your beauty. Empowered beauty. Clean, whole, rejoicing.

Of all acts of man, repentance is the most divine.
THOMAS CARLYLE

71

Repentance to Gain Holy and Peaceful Strength

I suddenly felt stronger.
DANIEL 10:19

How do we spell repentance? R-e-l-e-a-s-e. That's the sweet spot of repentance.

Rather than feel worse when we acknowledge sin, we feel better. Rather than feel grungy and awful, we feel clean and blessed. Rather than feel tied in knots and burdened, we feel strong. Peaceful and strong.

Daniel described the wonder of this release. "I suddenly felt stronger."

Indeed, after confessing the sins of his people to God, fasting from rich foods (meats and wine)—and even from fragrant lotions for his skin—he was blessed with a vision. Anguished and weak from such a sight, he could barely breathe from his feelings. But the vision, of a man, encouraged him:

"Don't be afraid," he said, "for you are very precious to God" (v. 19).

Then a sweet spot.

"Peace!" the man said.

But there was more:

"Be encouraged!" the man added. "Be strong!" (v. 19).

Wonderful words, aren't they? Surely God knows our struggle with sin, and our bigger struggle to confess it. Disclosing our cover-ups, denials, blinders, and lies exhausts even the best of us. Yet when we acknowledge our faults to Him, shining the light of truth on them—with courage and honesty—He blesses us with peaceful strength.

Whatever emotional effort it took to open our mouths and confess our offenses, He blesses with His grace.

Awesome God. In fact: "There is no condemnation," the apostle Paul wrote, "for those who belong to Christ Jesus. And because you belong to him, the power of the life-giving Spirit has freed you from the power of sin that leads to death" (Romans 8:1-2).

That's release. Repent today and receive this precious and beautiful gift. His Name is Jesus.

When we deal seriously with our sins,
God will deal gently with us.
CHARLES SPURGEON

72

Passion and Zeal for Spiritual Gifts

_As they listen . . . they will fall to
their knees and worship God._

1 CORINTHIANS 14:25

Love your job—or hate it? Love your life—or
filled with regrets? Passion for your life, ideals,
vocation—and also faith—fuels a heart that makes
a difference.

But the apostle Paul urges believers to be passionate, not just for jobs or lives, but first for "the special
abilities" the Spirit gives us, especially the gift of
prophecy (1 Corinthians 12:1, 10).

Prophecy? But wait.

What about passion for our artistry? For our
carpentry or baking or software engineering or
designing or doctoring or for any other God-given
gift we may enjoy? What, indeed, about the idea that
passion "makes all things alive," as poet Ralph Waldo
Emerson says? All good, Paul would say. But the
apostle brings us back to ground with this reminder:

Be passionate first for the gifts of the Holy Spirit, in whatever form they take. Why? They build up the church and encourage the love of God.

But what kind of church, and what kind of people, would need such a reminder? The lukewarm church at Laodicea needed it (Revelation 3:15). Same for the church at Corinth. But neither church was that much different from many today.

So Paul teaches this: Love is better. Prophecy is better. When people come into our churches— feeling our love and hearing our revelation of God's Word—"their secret thoughts will be exposed, and they will fall to their knees and worship God, declaring, 'God is truly here among you'" (1 Corinthians 14:25).

But you don't hunger for love or prophecy? Pray for it. Not sure you've been bestowed with a spiritual gift? Pray for it to be revealed. Then use what the Holy Spirit gives you. Not to make yourself look good—but to point another hungry person to the Cross.

God requires that His gifts should be sought for.
ARTHUR PINK

73

Passion and Zeal for Giving Offerings

God loves a person who gives cheerfully.
2 CORINTHIANS 9:7

The offering basket passes by and you cringe. Or you dig deep in your wallet and pour in generously. Either way, wrote Paul, giving in church isn't so much about the money. Instead, giving money for Christian ministry reflects how much you and I have given ourselves to Christ.

But money is the test.

Paul knew that. So in his second letter to the church at Corinth, he wrote two whole chapters about giving—including a piercing reminder: Dragging our feet to give won't bless anybody.

"I want it to be a willing gift, not one given grudgingly" (9:5).

Paul gently said that, reminding them that poverty-stricken believers in Jerusalem needed their help. But church members in Corinth, after starting to give, had slacked off. (Sound familiar?) Even

146

a "poorer" church in Macedonia had given beyond their share, Paul wrote.

Now what about you?

Paul's question rings down through history right to your pew. Is your ministry of giving so generous and cheerful, trusting and passionate—so based, not on what you have, but on who God is—that others are blessed by your passion to give?

Put down your checkbook when you answer such a question. Look, instead, at the Macedonian believers. Despite dire poverty, they dug deep. Giving beyond their own ability, they trusted God to bless *and* restore their gifts.

Can you give with such zeal, believing, as Paul wrote, that "you will be enriched in every way so that you can always be generous" (v. 11)? You'll give like that if your giving is inspired not by money—but by trust.

What does it look like? Audacious love.

Passion will move men beyond themselves.
JOE CAMPBELL

74

Strength and Vigor from God Alone

*Power and might are in your hand, and at your
discretion people are made great and given strength.*

As a child, I loved Popeye cartoons. Those
spinach-eating scenes, where a can of the green
stuff morphed into big biceps, always made me
giggle. Nothing is funny, however, about the health
risk of muscle-building steroids. From liver damage
and high blood pressure, to infertility and mood
shifts, clear dangers face abusers of such drugs.

So why would anybody use them?

To look better? Feel stronger? Gain confidence?

Or could the problem be spiritual?

When any of us seek strength from any source
other than God, aren't we giving in to the myth that
strength can be bought, consumed, or manipulated?

King David understood this. At the coronation
of his son Solomon, he praised God alone for being
the source of our strength. More amazing, however,

David didn't ask God to grant His strength to God's people.

Instead, David prayed for obedience. "Make your people always want to obey you" (1 Chronicles 29:18). Strength will come from God, as He chooses to give it. But obedience blesses us first.

That's still true today. Bulking up with drugs to get strong won't help us. Begging God for strength won't empower us. We bless God, instead, by seeking to obey Him. As we obey, we'll find ourselves empowered with the Spirit of His love.

We are a long time in learning that all our strength and salvation is in God.
DAVID BRAINERD

75

Creativity through Obedience to God

Build a large boat from cypress wood.
GENESIS 6:14

The great myth about creativity? That it's free-flowing, over the top, out of the box.

But as all effective artists and performers know, creativity follows obedience. That's true for painters, sculptors, chefs, writers, tailors, carpenters, web designers—any creative type. Breaking rules doesn't happen with much success until basic rules are learned and followed.

Thus, Noah could've built any old kind of boat.

But as a righteous man, Noah obeyed when God provided *His* blueprint.

"Construct decks and stalls throughout its interior," the Lord told Noah. "Make the boat 450 feet long, 75 feet wide, and 45 feet high. Leave an 18-inch opening below the roof all the way around the boat. Put the door on the side, and build three decks inside the boat—lower, middle, and upper" (vv. 14-16).

Talk about exact directions.

Noah never even questioned God about the boat or the building of it. That's true even though such a boat—a long, rectangular barge, says the *NLT Study Bible*—was "for survival, not for navigation." The eighteen-inch opening below the roof "provid[ed] light and air." With no sail or rudder, the boat would be navigated by God, its true captain.

Closely attuned to God, Noah simply listened to the Creator's plan and followed, reflecting Psalm 19:7: "The instructions of the LORD are perfect. . . . the decrees of the LORD are trustworthy."

If your creativity suffers, try aiming for more obedience to God—in your art, but first in your life. Sure, you may not be building a big boat. But obey God. He is the Creator. The thumbprint of His Word will anoint your creative efforts with blessed grace. Because you're talented? No, because you obey.

---

*Biblically speaking, the making of art
is not an option but a command.*
HAROLD BEST

76

Unity in Harmony with Other Believers

Then all of you can join together with one voice.
ROMANS 15:6

I sing second alto. On good days, I sing second alto. On great days, however, I follow the choirmaster. Yet here I was on this day, singing the wrong note—harmonizing on my own, but not following the music with the others.

"That's a C-*flat*," the experienced first alto said to me. It was my first rehearsal in a renowned community choir, so I was singing by ear. The first alto smiled, but I could see her displeasure. Sing it *right*, her look was saying.

I shifted in my chair, feeling her disapproval.

Later, however, thinking about her reaction, I understood. If every choir member sang a wrong note, the choir's sound would be noisy chaos.

But there was more to this matter of harmony.

After a few rehearsals, I finally saw: Even if every member sings the right notes, the sound is a mess if we don't follow the choir director in unity.

She stood before us. Waiting for us to put down our music and *watch her.* If you learn your notes at home, she was saying, when we sing together "you can follow me."

So I went home and learned my music. Back at rehearsal, I could put down the paper and raise my eyes to look. Trying to follow the director. Trying to hear Paul's lesson to the various early churches all over Rome's provinces: "May God . . . help you live in complete harmony with each other, as is fitting for followers of Christ Jesus" (Romans 15:5). Then?

"Then all of you can join together with one voice, giving praise and glory to God, the Father of our Lord Jesus Christ" (v. 6).

We could ignore Paul. Or not look at Christ. Or we could work on our unity. We'll look better. We'll get more done. More than anything, we'll sound better. Then what will our unity sound like to the world's listeners? A praise song to the choirmaster.

I feel a part of the congregation.
I've never had to do special music.
AMY GRANT

77

Unity within Our Local Church

He makes the whole body fit together perfectly.
EPHESIANS 4:16

What's the sign of disunity in a church? It's not pretty.

"Quarreling, jealousy, anger, selfishness, slander, gossip, arrogance, and disorderly behavior."

That is Paul's list from 2 Corinthians 12:20. Paul's concern, when he arrived at the church at Corinth, was that he'd find this hornets' nest of trouble and more. "And I will be grieved," he wrote, "because many of you have not given up your old sins. You have not repented of your impurity, sexual immorality, and eagerness for lustful pleasure" (v. 21).

Talk about a church mess.

A church in disunity has lost its center.

Jesus is pushed to the corners.

Paul warned of this danger to yet another church, at Ephesus. Paul's tactic was to name, one by one, the different gifts given by Christ to the church: apostles, prophets, evangelists, pastors, and teachers (Ephesians 4:11).

154

Their job? "To equip God's people to do his work and build up the church" (v. 12).

A big job, indeed. "This will continue until we all come to such unity in our faith and knowledge of God's Son that we will be mature in the Lord, measuring up to the full and complete standard of Christ" (v. 13).

But in the meantime? Disunity runs rampant in some churches as Jesus is pushed to the corners—and sometimes right out the door.

In such settings, however, the way back to unity is through the one who "makes the whole body fit together perfectly" (v. 16). In Christ, ugly turns to grace and ashes turn to beauty; the broken no longer divided but unified. Will we let Him do this work in our hearts today? If so, we'll see the blessing and evidence in church. And the world?

The world will see the One.

He is the Peace that is above every estrangement and cleavage and faction.
KARL BARTH

78

Wisdom for a Blessed Life

Getting wisdom is the wisest thing you can do! And whatever else you do, develop good judgment.
PROVERBS 4:7

At eighty-five, my uncle had notched many years on the belt called life. So he didn't panic while I ranted on about my then-favorite topic—the problem of race relations in America.

We were sitting in my mother's kitchen and I was raging—hurting from a past filled with too many put-downs and slights, too much name-calling and nay-saying. Even in Colorado, where I grew up, the ugly stamp of racism had tainted my fifties childhood enough to make me, thirtysomething at that point, not just feel hate, but nurture it. So, as I saw it, I had plenty to gripe about when it came to race.

But my uncle, who was born and reared in the South—and still lived there at that visit—looked across my mother's kitchen table and gave me a patient smile.

"You can't hate people, Patricia," he said.

A voice of wisdom. Hard-earned wisdom.

I looked at him, searching his eyes. They were aging but resolved.

"If you hate," he went on, "the only person it will hurt will be you."

I sat tight lipped, agitated but listening. Considering. Hearing. Knowing he was right, and needing somebody to finally say what he was telling me: Love never fails.

My uncle's words, in fact, saved my life. In a few years, I would take his words to heart and strike out on a journey that would lead me to write a book on racial forgiveness, *My First White Friend*, then travel across the nation promoting forgiveness. Even better, that journey taught me that to love others, I could start with myself. His wise words changed my life, that is.

When I consider, indeed, the power of wisdom, I think of this moment in my late mother's kitchen when a beloved uncle cared enough about his niece to share what a lifetime had taught him: Love is better than hate. A pearl of wisdom. Its value? Priceless.

I've decided to stick with love.
Hate is too great a burden to bear.
MARTIN LUTHER KING JR.

79

Wisdom for Safety

Wise choices will watch over you.
Understanding will keep you safe.

Proverbs 2:11

What is the best wisdom you've ever heard?
Priceless, perfect, and on time?

For me, the words are stamped on my heart.
You need to open your Bible.

My daddy said these words. I was just twenty-three, but I was divorcing a husband. I was a young mother with a two-year-old child. I was jobless, despite a new college degree. And I was broke, a prodigal daughter come home for atonement and renewal in my good parents' home.

Come on back, they said. So I went.

Then they did the remarkable. They never once said "we told you so." They just put up a crib in my old bedroom, bought baby food and diapers, ordered nursery books and toys. Then my daddy, a tall brown man with strong arms and quiet ways, spoke in his true voice the words that would change my life. "You need to open your Bible."

Nothing more. No fancy words. No fussing or lectures. On that morning, Daddy just quietly left me in his living room, giving me a choice. So I lifted the big Bible from its place on my parents' coffee table and I opened it, surprised that the words of my recovery had been underlined years before with my daddy's black-ink fountain pen.

There is therefore now no condemnation to those who are in Christ Jesus (Romans 8:1, NKJV).

I saw my daddy's past, linked up with my mother's dreams, all tied together with my future and underscored in ink years before by my father's hopeful hand.

And we know that all things work together for good to them that love God.

Through fresh tears, I dared then to ask God to work good in me. Looking back, I can say that He answered. But first came wise words. Just a few.

Wisdom is not wordy.
GARY AMIRAULT

80

Wisdom with Great Joy

Joyful is the person who finds wisdom.
PROVERBS 3:13

J oy and wisdom. A pair of soul mates? Could that be right?

In fact, we find in our Bibles promise after promise linking the two together. *Joyful is the person who finds wisdom.*

Even a onetime mention would have caught my attention. But I look closer and there it is again (italics added to each verse below):

"For wisdom will enter your heart, and knowledge will fill you with *joy*" (Proverbs 2:10).

Then again:

"The man who loves wisdom brings *joy* to his father" (Proverbs 29:3).

Then again:

"God gives wisdom, knowledge, and *joy* to those who please him" (Ecclesiastes 2:26).

This last reference is especially compelling. The book of Ecclesiastes, filled as it is with sorrow and melancholy and joy, eventually settles on the importance of balance in life. As the *NLT Study Bible* puts it: "It is exactly this balance of joy and sorrow that characterizes the wise person who reflects on all of life and understands its complexities in a fallen world."

Life is tough, indeed. At its worst, it can feel unbearable.

But those who pursue the wisdom of God will arrive, despite troubles, at joy.

Do we see the extraordinary lesson?

In the midst of troubles, we do not pursue their solution—but we pursue wisdom in the midst of the trials. Then what do we experience? God's joy.

Seems illogical. But our wisdom pursuit blesses God. Then He blesses us with joy.

Joy is the serious business of Heaven.
C. S. Lewis

81

Courage to Face the Fearsome

*God is our refuge and strength, always
ready to help in times of trouble.*

PSALM 46:1

Trapped under seven hundred thousand tons of
solid rock—half a mile underground for sixty-
nine days—thirty-three miners in Chile endure their
weeks-long ordeal in the summer of 2010 with real
courage? But how?

I ask this question while watching on TV, along
with millions around the world, as rescuers lift the
miners, one by one, to safety. Afterward, days will go
by before the miners meet TV cameras or give inter-
views or write books to shed light on their ordeal.

But as I watch, gaping with awe at the fuzzy
TV picture of the solid rock that entrapped them,
I believe I find my answer for their courage.

Those miners must've realized that the solid
rock wasn't their tomb. It was their fortress. (*Rock* in
Hebrew means "fortress.") So while they waited for
rescue, the solid rock surrounding them wasn't their
enemy, but their strength.

Indeed, this solid rock was Jesus—their defense and shelter, their refuge and keeping-power deliverance.

Jesus' tomb, indeed, wasn't His grave, but our door—our Door to abundant life.

Psalm 46 reveals this perspective. So if you're feeling trapped today, encased in what feels like a solid tomb of trouble, let the words of this powerful psalm turn your entrapment into courage. How? By knowing this:

God *is* our refuge and strength. "The God of Israel is our fortress" (v. 11).

Shielded by His strong arms of safety, get up and wait for His rescue with confidence, and even with joy. Losing hope? Think of thirty-three miners, waiting under solid rock and singing—Elvis Presley songs and hymns—for their deliverance.

Then sing Psalm 46, letting its words of assurance bless you to the core with rock-solid courage.

Rock of Ages, cleft for me,
Let me hide myself in thee.
AUGUSTUS M. TOPLADY

82

Courage to Believe and Serve God

∽◦∾

As she listened to us, the Lord opened her heart.
ACTS 16:14

What makes a fireman run into a burning building?

What makes a soldier face enemy fire to rescue a fallen soldier?

What makes a schoolkid stand up for a child facing bullies on a playground?

We see the answer in the Bible story of Lydia. A wealthy merchant of purple cloth, rich enough to own a nice home, she is mentioned in only two short passages in the Bible.

As she listened with other women to Paul and Silas talk about Jesus, the Lord "opened her heart" and she accepted what Paul was saying. Then she took a risk.

Without any recorded hesitation, she invited Paul and Silas to stay in her home.

Despite the risk of harboring a controversial religious apostle.

Despite the potential costs to her business.

Despite the possible physical threats she may have faced.

What made her open her home despite it all?

She believed in the Lord—yes, in the Cross of Christ and its power to redeem.

Such belief undergirds every moral stand and physical risk ever taken by a believer. Thus, belief is why Queen Esther risked all to speak to the king on behalf of her Jewish people. It's why Lydia opened her home. Why Harriet Tubman risked capture to free slaves and why Rosa Parks refused to sit at the back of a segregated bus. Why Jim Elliot and four other missionaries risked their lives in the jungles of Ecuador to witness to a primitive tribe that killed them. It's why, indeed, Elliot's wife, Elisabeth, returned to the jungle, later living with the same tribe that killed her husband.

Standing on belief, these courageous believers served. Now in what do we believe? We can answer the question by blessing God with a clear, firm answer. Then may God help us to stand up and live our answers.

There is nothing worth living for,
unless it is worth dying for.
ELISABETH ELLIOT

83

Persistence to Hold On to Faith

But the one who endures to the end will be saved.
MATTHEW 24:13

Don't give up. So easy to say. Just three little words. So Jesus, to be sure, knew it was easier said than done. He even warned His disciples about what was coming: Wars and rumors of wars. Nations warring against nations. Famine and earthquakes all over the world. Even more, "you will be arrested, persecuted, and killed" (Matthew 24:9).

Could it get any worse for these fledgling followers? Or for us?

Some days we feel defeated, as if we're hanging by a thread, swinging by a sliver of lint on a proverbial rope. Other days every anti-Christian power in the world seems to scream in our faces, with a rage that reminds us of what Jesus predicted:

We will be hated. Sin will be rampant. Love will turn cold. False prophets will preach and self-promote. Believers will be killed. That and more can be expected for those who profess Christ.

When our faith walk seems at its lowest, however, and when it feels senseless to profess a faith that the whole world seems to ridicule, question, and attack, *don't give up.*

When prayers seem to go unanswered and problems seem to get worse, not better, *don't give up.*

When obstacles grow higher and land mines explode louder, *don't give up.*

Those three little words would seem not enough to keep us going.

But Jesus Himself spoke this sentiment—and He still speaks: "The one who endures to the end will be saved." Saved from what? From every enemy. Every attack. Every disappointment. Every challenge. Every battle, burden, and betrayal.

So let's open our hearts today to the beautiful blessing of His promise: Faith in Christ still saves the lost, but first the faithful.

A little hail and wind can't run me off.
WILLIAM NOTTER

84

Persistence in Living Right

*So let's not get tired of doing what is
good. At just the right time we will reap a
harvest of blessing if we don't give up.*

GALATIANS 6:9

In our spiritual liberty, Christians can be tempted
to justify sin.

I'll be forgiven anyway.

My salvation is safe.

*I harvest so much fruit, any sin I commit isn't that
big a deal.*

We can justify all day and all night. We can twist
our freedom in Christ so far we're able to qualify
almost any act, arguing that we're "covered" by the
blood and by faith . . . and, well, we know how such
arguments can go.

Especially if others are sinning. And especially if
those others are sitting right there in church—sitting
in the next pew—or even sinning in the next pew.

But don't be misled. Paul writes in Galatians 6:7,
"You will always harvest what you plant." Sin, that
is, only reaps "decay and death" (v. 8).

Sure, we in Christ are forgiven. Sure, we're saved by faith and not works. Sure, we're covered by the blood. But sin always kills—our hopes and dreams. Families and friendships. Bodies and minds. Churches and neighborhoods. Communities and nations.

Sin always kills.

So don't get tired of doing what is good.

Seems obvious, doesn't it? As people of faith and followers of Christ, our commitment to righteous living should be a given. But Paul cautions us. Don't take right living for granted. Deliberately, instead, stick with right.

When we get tired, stick with right. When sin is easier, stick with right. Let the Holy Spirit lead the way, but stick with right. Then, at the right time, Paul writes, we'll reap a harvest of blessing, grown in the beautiful soil of His persistent grace.

The best way to fight against sin is
to fight it on our knees.
PHILIP HENRY

85

Persistence in Seeking God

*Search for the LORD and for his strength;
continually seek him.*

1 CHRONICLES 16:11

Whom did King Saul seek when he needed
guidance? The troubled leader of Israel
turned to a medium for wisdom. That means Saul
sought a soothsayer who claimed to talk to spirits
communicating with the dead.

No kidding.

The first king of Israel, who could have persistently sought God Almighty Himself for divine
guidance on every aspect of his life, "consulted a
medium instead of asking the LORD for guidance"
(1 Chronicles 10:13-14).

So he died in shame, the chronicler says, falling
on his own sword.

Then came King David. A man after God's own
heart, David exhorted the Israelites to search, not for
mediums, but "for the LORD." Continually.

Or in the words of the King James translation

of the Holy Bible: "Seek the LORD and his strength, seek his face continually." Persistently, indeed.

This isn't idle advice. Not then. Not now.

David knew personally how Saul turned from seeking God to seeking other sources of help. The result? Saul's life went from good to bad to worse. A promising leader with greater potential, Saul ended up a miserable, despised, dead failure.

His mistake? Talking to spirits. Thus disobeying God.

Are you hearing this today? Embracing the Bible promise—that those who seek God continually *lack no good thing*? Are you seeking continually, not psychic spirits, but God's Holy Spirit—your Comforter and your Help? Seeking the Lord continually, indeed, for the best reason ever—because He may be found? How?

Continually. Persistently. So don't give up. Then as we keep seeking, He will bless.

The art of love is largely the art of persistence.
ALBERT ELLIS

86

Hard Work That's Empowered and Inspired by God

And the Spirit of the LORD came powerfully upon David from that day on.

1 SAMUEL 16:13

Why do some people succeed on the job? And others fail? Do such questions stir up nagging, uncomfortable emotions?

In fact, four of five people are in the wrong job, some experts say. Others manage to love their work and thrive in it. Says film communications expert Ted Baehr in his book *So You Want to Be in Pictures*: "These findings . . . are nothing more than an affirmation of the fact that God has designed each of us for a particular purpose."

In fact, says Baehr, God "wants us to be joyous and enjoy our work." And if you don't? Go on a prayer journey with God to find out why.

As you examine your life in prayer, you are likely to see clear evidence of the special gifts and talents granted to you by God. For "all authority comes from God," says Romans 13:1, and "a spiritual gift is given to each of us so we can help each other" (1 Corinthians 12:7).

A Spirit-filled life, in other words, dignifies whatever honest work we do. But will we work hard and stick to godly values—despite delays and discouragement—until God inspires a Spirit-filled breakthrough? So we can help each other?

To be sure, hard work is exactly that. Hard. Work. But God's blessed Holy Spirit empowers us to keep going, during downturns and more. That's what happened to David. Life after his anointing as king was hardly smooth sailing. The current king, Saul, kept trying to kill him. After Saul's death, everybody from David's wife to his son conspired to bring him down.

But empowered by God's Spirit, David overcame every obstacle that confronted him at work—including his own sin. Are you overwhelmed by work, by being in the wrong job, or by not having a job? Pray for God's Spirit to direct your job journey. Then work hard to help others. It's a combination that God will grace with His power.

When love and skill work together, expect a masterpiece.
JOHN RUSKIN

87

Hard Work as unto the Lord

*Remember that the Lord will give you
an inheritance as your reward.*

COLOSSIANS 3:24

I needed a tile layer. A good tile layer. A trustworthy tile layer. I wasn't afraid, in fact, to pray for exactly that for our old-school bathroom.

So there he was. A young man. A fellow church member. He posted on Facebook photos of tile work he'd just completed. He bragged, in fact, about one job he'd done, noting "how level and flat this 300 square feet of tile is. We pride ourselves on good work!"

Praise the Lord. Good work. That's precisely what I needed.

Good work. It seems so hard to find these days. A worker who shows up on time. A worker who finishes on time. Who doesn't steal—like the subcontractor we hired once who didn't pay his workers, so they came back for more money, forcing us to pay twice.

Good work. *Please, God.* I prayed hard.

Then the young man from church showed up, ready to work. And on time.

As I told him, "I just want it done right."

He smiled, showing me that "done right" was his watchword.

Still, I joked. Or tried to. "It'll be right because you'll see me at church every Sunday." He smiled again. "Nope," he said.

He looked me in the eye. "It will be right because I have to answer to Him."

He pointed upward, showing me what I needed to see. *I'm working for Him.*

As unto the Lord.

Paul taught this principle to new believers—that we work willingly and sincerely, "at whatever [we] do," in reverent fear of the Lord, "as though [we] were working for the Lord rather than for people" (v. 23). Our young tile worker did exactly that. May God bless him, but also us, to work this same perfect way on this day. The reward? An inheritance of life in Him.

The work done by a worshiper will have eternity in it.
A. W. TOZER

88

Order and Discipline: Starting with Small Things

*If you are faithful in little things,
you will be faithful in large ones.*

LUKE 16:10

Fold the laundry. Wash the dishes. Make the bed. Clean the desk. Wax the car. Say thank you. Smile. Open a door. Say you're welcome. Little things.

Writing about such matters in *The Pillars of Christian Character*, John MacArthur makes this solid point: "Learning self-discipline in the little things of life prepares the way for big successes."

That's quite a promise. But as this author argues: "Those who are undisciplined in small matters will likely be undisciplined in more important issues."

Jesus understands this perfectly. Teaching His disciples this principle, He tells a curious story about a shrewd manager who earns favors for life by dishonestly rewarding his friends. An odd story from Jesus, yes—until we reflect on the rich truth of His point:

If even a dishonest man knows to plan for the

long length of his life, we who are promised eternal life must start planning for it in even small things.

For "if you are faithful in little things, you will be faithful in large ones." As Jesus adds: "If you are untrustworthy about worldly wealth, who will trust you with the true riches of heaven?" (v. 11).

So I made a list. Small things. Things I'd let pass that needed regular attention.

Hug my husband. Call my neighbor. Balance checkbook. Floss. Walk. Stay on top of those dishes! Then a curious thing happened. The more little things I gave regular attention to, thanking God for the privilege, the better I got at handling bigger things.

At seeing what other people needed—and providing it. At going to weekly Bible study—and learning from it. At valuing other people's time—and acting like it. Takes effort? Yes. But the effort lets God trust me with true riches. That's the glory, indeed, of such a path. Everybody can start such a journey. Why not bless God today by taking the small first step?

True freedom in any area of life is the consequence of regular discipline.
Sinclair B. Ferguson

89

Order and Discipline in All Thoughts

Think about things that are excellent and worthy of praise. . . . Then the God of peace will be with you.

PHILIPPIANS 4:8-9

A church friend was in the hospital. So I decided to visit to pray. But immediately the doubts rose to attack. What would I say? How would I pray? I thought hard on the matter, deciding to go in faith, but also in confidence. So praying boldly, I turned off the light and went to sleep, prepared to meet my friend the next day.

Then the attack. About 3 a.m., an hour when I'm typically fast asleep, I woke with an awful dream. It dredged up an old family issue. I sighed, tossing about for a few anxious moments, almost waking my husband. Then I stopped.

Think about things that are excellent and worthy of praise.

I'd copied that Scripture that same day while writing about order and discipline in our spiritual lives. So I recalled Paul's reminder to the church at

Philippi, hearing as I lay in the dark the old King James wording: "Finally, brethren, whatsoever things are true, whatsoever things are honest, whatsoever things are just, whatsoever things are pure, whatsoever things are lovely, whatsoever things are of good report; if there be any virtue, and if there be any praise, *think on these things*" (italics added).

So that's what I did. *O true and honest God,* I spoke in my spirit, *if this dream is not of You, remove it from my mind right now.*

I didn't wait for an answer. With confident discipline, I started instead right then to think about God—and His truth, goodness, honesty, justice, purity, loveliness, and power. In seconds, the dream and its disturbing images faded, then vanished. Soon I slept in peace.

Some trick of the mind? Or did I bless God by obeying His order to discipline our minds to think of good? To answer, let's bless Him today by turning our thinking to His good. What will follow? His disciplined goodness. His ordered love. His blessed confidence. His powerful peace.

With complete consecration comes perfect peace.
WATCHMAN NEE

90

Order and Discipline in All Speech

Those who control their tongue will have a long life.

PROVERBS 13:3

If you can't say anything nice . . . Don't we all know the rest of *that* classic adage?

Don't say anything at all.

We've all heard this. Mostly from parents. Often from Sunday school teachers. From friends. From loved ones. Surely from the Word of God itself.

But, oh, that tongue. Talk about *un*disciplined. James is so right. It's "a flame of fire. It is a whole world of wickedness, corrupting your entire body. It can set your whole life on fire, for it is set on fire by hell itself" (James 3:6).

In fact, no one can tame it, James declares. "It is restless and evil, full of deadly poison"—pouring forth both praises of our Lord and Father, but also curses toward "those who have been made in the image of God" (James 3:8-9). Does that describe our tongues? Full of conflicting noise—both praises *and* curses?

The habit isn't just unpleasant. It shortens our lives, says God's Word. Stirring up heat and hate. Injuring others, but also ourselves. Revealing a cold heart—or making it colder.

Kind words, in contrast, "are like honey—sweet to the soul and healthy for the body" (Proverbs 16:24). For all the effort modern humans give to eating right and exercising, we'd all do ourselves more good by taming our tongues. But how?

Give our tongues to God's Spirit. Let's bless God, that is, by using our tongues today to ask for what they need most—the power of God's Spirit for control.

"Each of you," says the apostle Peter in Acts 2:38, "must repent of your sins and turn to God, and be baptized in the name of Jesus Christ for the forgiveness of your sins. *Then you will receive the gift of the Holy Spirit*" (italics added), to be used, in part, to control our tongues. It's the gift of life, indeed—this gift of a Spirit-led tongue. Let's bless God today and ask for it.

Focus on your mouth. . . . The rest will be subdued.
JOHN MACARTHUR

91

Order and Discipline in Our Finances

For God loves a person who gives cheerfully.
2 CORINTHIANS 9:7

Living paycheck to paycheck, I spent thirty working years frustrated by money. With every paycheck, money flew in one door and out the next. So I prayed. Finally. The right prayer? I asked God to show me the secrets of personal money management. Pretty good prayer? Apparently, because while talking about my crisis to my-daughter-the-accountant, she spoke the word that changed my financial life: budget.

"Budget?"

"Make a budget, Mom," she said. "For every year, month, day. Decide what you have to spend, what you need to spend—then budget accordingly."

She made it sound so simple. "Simple accounting, yes," she agreed. So I tried it.

And my life changed.

Not just my financial life. My *life* changed. Money management is that important. I finally appreciated my frugal dad's commitment to live beneath his income—save and invest the difference—then give back to God generously. So while others bought fancy cars and houses, Daddy and Mama bought plain. He went to glory without debt. So did my mama.

So, while living, they gave to God generously, cheerfully. And God *loves* a person who gives cheerfully. Oh, it took me so long to see this truth.

Discipline in financial matters allows us, not to hoard up money, but to steward it so wisely we always have enough to give back to God. Cheerfully.

And God loves that. Those who give back to Him trust Him. "It is more blessed to give," Jesus said, "than to receive" (Acts 20:35). But what allows such blessed giving? Knowing and loving God enough to discipline our stewardship.

Does it matter how much money is involved? Never. One penny managed well for God is a fortune. What matters is our disciplined honor of God's provision so we can give it back cheerfully. Oh, how this blesses God—not to mention empowering us.

We are not cisterns made for hoarding;
we are channels made for sharing.

BILLY GRAHAM

92

Perseverance in Believing God

〰️

*At just the right time we will reap a
harvest of blessing if we don't give up.*
GALATIANS 6:9

George Müller. Let's put his name on the table. Right on top. In any talk about perseverance, Müller surely stands with the best. His familiar story of redemption, inspiration, and endurance in prayer deserves regular retelling, to be sure.

So here's Müller, a ne'er-do-well gambler and thief. As young as ten, say biographers, he was stealing government money from his father, a Prussian tax collector. At fourteen, while his mother lay dying, he was playing cards and drinking with friends.

Then came Jesus. Healing, restoring, forgiving Jesus. So Müller, seeing he needed salvation, gave his life to Christ—eventually working with his wife to start orphanages that would feed, educate, and house some ten thousand homeless, hungry children in Bristol, England. How'd Müller do it?

With prayer. Enduring, persevering, stubborn, never-give-up prayer.

For all his faith in a providing God, Müller must best be remembered for his determined, persistent, unwavering prayers to the God who meets needs in time.

Even for the starving. So while Müller said grace for breakfast, when he had no breakfast, this persevering servant led his wife and the orphans in thanking God for what they were about to receive, just as a baker knocked on the door—with enough fresh breakfast bread for all. Müller never asked others for anything, in fact. He only asked God.

So Müller prayed enduringly over fifty-two years for five former pals to accept Christ. Sure enough, one by one each came to the Lord—including the last friend who came to Jesus at Müller's funeral.

Give up? Müller, crying out across history, says no. Keep trying. Keep praying. Keep blessing God. Keep letting Him inspire and save. How? Don't stop believing.

Patient, persevering, believing prayer, offered up to God, in the name of the Lord Jesus, has always, sooner or later, brought the blessing.
GEORGE MÜLLER

93

Temperance in Our Lifestyles

*Enjoy what you have rather than
desiring what you don't have.*

ECCLESIASTES 6:9

We can't shop our way to happiness. So why do people keep trying? In fact, psychologists insist that having more, buying more, and experiencing more don't make people happier. Experts even have a fancy name to explain the problem—"hedonic adaptation." It means that when things improve in our lives (we get more money, fancy cars, bigger houses, success in work or missions), we soon become used to such things.

After a brief boost in happiness, our happiness levels sink back to "normal."

So those who chase bigger payoffs soon find they need yet more payoff to feel better. (Psychologists call this the "hedonic treadmill.")

It's as King Solomon wrote: "Those who love pleasure become poor; wine and luxury are not the way to riches" (Proverbs 21:17). Tempering our consumption, instead, enriches our happiness.

Instinctively, it seems, we all understand that less *is* more.

So tempering our lusts for luxuries—in whatever form—grants the peace and pleasure we were seeking all along. To know, for example, that drug use in the United States is higher than in any other nation tells us something about this hedonistic paradox. (Americans have the highest levels of lifetime illegal cocaine and marijuana use and the highest rate of lifetime tobacco use in the world.)

We can be absolutely confident, however, in the Bible's reminder that "it is better to have little with fear for the LORD than to have great treasure with turmoil" (Proverbs 15:16).

In fact, the best things in life—loving relationships, good health, purpose, the beauty of nature—are free. So let us temper our craving for more. The blessing? The empowered surprise of joy in Him.

God is always better than gold.
JOHN PIPER

94

Vigilance to Guard Our Hearts from Temptation

*Keep watch and pray, so that you will not give in to
temptation. For the spirit is willing, but the body is weak!*
MATTHEW 26:41

Of course the vigilant get blessed. And not just
sometimes. Daily they flee temptation, turn
from sin, defeat disappointment, outlast terror, shun
evil, keep covenants, walk in righteousness, never
give up. And all that from keeping their eyes wide
open for Christ as they pray.

They're wise, in other words, knowing that
keeping watch for Jesus protects them from Satan—
the same enemy who deceived Eve with his "cunning
ways" (2 Corinthians 11:3), who prowls around
constantly, working overtime to distract us with his
devilish, sneaky lies.

But is he prowling with success? Only if we're
not watching. Our enemy celebrates, in fact, when
we're asleep with weakness, our truest nature. But it
was Jesus who described it perfectly: "For from the

heart come evil thoughts, murder, adultery, all sexual immorality, theft, lying, and slander. These are what defile you."

When Christ spoke these words in Matthew 15:19-20, He was talking to Peter, explaining to His disciple why true inner purity matters more than the ritual purity of hand washing or eating "clean" food.

Inner purity results from a heart that shuns its temptations, choosing instead to honor God by walking in His ways—not chasing lusts, breaking trusts, or snoozing.

So keep watch.

But don't just keep watch. Leap up today and pray—as if it's a matter of life and death, because it is. Indeed, are family members failing? Leap up and pray. Are church numbers falling? Leap up and pray. Ignore Satan's lie that watching and praying don't matter. Such vigilance saves lives and souls. So keep watch. Every minute. Every second, too. Then let the Holy Spirit bless you with His victorious presence as you watch, awake in Him, and vigilantly pray.

The safe place lies in obedience to God's Word,
singleness of heart and holy vigilance.
A. B. SIMPSON

95

Vigilance to Watch for the Blessings of Battle

Be careful! Watch out for attacks from the Devil, your great enemy. He prowls around like a roaring lion, looking for some victim to devour.

1 PETER 5:8

Watch for Jesus? We know to do that. But are we watching as hard for His blessings?

I ask that question today with conviction.

Among some believers today, the push for humility and self-denial has left many teaching that it's wrong to look to God for *any* good favor or blessing.

Satan affirms this false teaching. Busying us with vain self-denial, pumping us up to feel superior about it while roaring in our ears with lies and doubts, he works hard at devouring our hope in God's golden promises to bless His people. Yet be not dismayed, because God "cares about what happens to you," Peter writes in verse 7. As members of His royal priesthood, we can cast our anxieties on Him—and get blessed in the process.

This would be good news for the Gentile audience of this letter. Like new believers of today, they struggled with persecution from those questioning their faith. They did not yet understand how struggle develops both character and courage.

And what's the blessing after struggle? "After you have suffered a little while, he will restore, support, and strengthen you, *and* he will place you on a firm foundation" (v. 10, italics added).

Resist the devil—then get blessed. We're restored and stronger. We're supported by God, and in Him granted a firm place to stand. At work. At home. In the world. Resist bad and get blessed for right.

To nonbelievers, as we battle, we may look square and nerdy, like weak "church people." But standing up to Satan is tough work. "From start to finish," said evangelist E. M. Bounds, "it is war."

God in His mercy, however, makes the fight worth it. So fight hard. But don't stop short of your blessing.

Never neglect details. When everyone's mind is dulled or distracted . . . be doubly vigilant.
Colin Powell

96

Commitment That Supports My Community

~&~

But all of you who were faithful to the LORD your God are still alive today—every one of you.

DEUTERONOMY 4:4

My next-door neighbor, a retired Marine, never breaks a promise. If I ask her to watch our house when I'm out of town, I return to a house that's still standing—but also with no pizza-shop flyers on the porch or stray newspapers cluttering the driveway.

She keeps promises. Then she goes the extra mile.

Even before the Marines, however, promises mattered to her. It seems she learned that from her father, who learned it from his father—who learned it during an era when a person's word was his bond. If somebody said it, you could count on it.

In God's Word, the book of Deuteronomy outlines the critical nature of such promise keeping. As we keep God's covenant, that is, obeying God's commandments and extending justice as God mandates, we "will live" (Deuteronomy 8:1) *and* enjoy "prosperous lives" (5:33) *and* "occupy the land" or territory God has promised (8:1), and enjoy all this *together*. As neighbors. As a nation.

So I sit with this idea today. Then I ask God to plant in my not-always-committed heart His amazing promise:

If I commit to do my small part, and so does everybody else, a whole nation prospers. "For what great nation has a god as near to them as the LORD our God is near to us whenever we call on him?" Moses asked. "And what great nation has decrees and regulations as righteous and fair as this body of instructions?" (Deuteronomy 4:7-8).

So how committed are you to your community, family, and God? Do you cut corners? Break promises? Go halfway? Tell half-truths? Say yes but do no? Talk big but act small? Or will you vow today to make promises you keep? By God's Spirit, a committed life can result. But the blessing won't only be yours. Everybody around you will praise God too.

We must not promise what we ought not,
lest we be called on to perform what we cannot.
ABRAHAM LINCOLN

97

Commitment That Reflects Christ's Life-Giving Spirit

Under the new covenant, the Spirit gives life.
2 CORINTHIANS 3:6

God doesn't make mistakes. So the old covenant between God and His people wasn't bad. And yet? "It lacked the power to enable people to do what it commanded," says my *NLT Study Bible.* That's surprising, but it's good and plain language. So I reflect on how the apostle Paul explained it: "The law of Moses was unable to save us because of the weakness of our sinful nature." So what did God do? "He sent his own Son in a body like the bodies we sinners have" (Romans 8:3).

I like this plain language, too. So I keep reading.

"And in that body God declared an end to sin's control over us by giving his Son as a sacrifice for our sins. He did this so that the just requirement of the law would be fully satisfied for us, who no longer follow our sinful nature but instead follow the Spirit" (Romans 8:3-4).

Yes, chasing after the Spirit. Then surrendering. That's how we finally commit to Christ.

So let go. Stop trying today, on your own, to obey those two great commandments: love God—and love everybody else as much as yourself.

Instead, by the power of God's Holy Spirit, allow God to help you love Him and others—becoming a minister of love, spreading God's love but also sharing His life.

"The old written covenant ends in death," says 2 Corinthians 3:6. "But under the new covenant, the Spirit gives life." Empowered but tender and wise and flexible and lasting life.

Does that describe your life yet? Or, by not following after His Spirit, are you failing at your commitment to enliven others through Christ? If so, pray for a fresh anointing of His Spirit. That's a prayer, indeed, that He won't turn down. So get ready to receive His answer—more Spirit-filled love and life—and the power to share it.

I myself do nothing. The Holy Spirit accomplishes all through me.
WILLIAM BLAKE

98

Service without Picking Favorites

*Since I, your Lord and Teacher, have washed
your feet, you ought to wash each other's feet.*

JOHN 13:14

Even Judas. The betrayer of Christ got his feet
washed too.

Even Judas. The one whose feet would run to
betrayal let Jesus wash off the dirt.

Even Judas, in that classic scene in the upper
room at the Passover meal, let Jesus scrub off grime.
To be sure, within hours, Judas would betray Jesus.
Yet Jesus put on a servant's towel and washed the feet
of all His disciples. Even Judas.

A small detail in this story? Or the most important?

This wondrous moment is always remembered
for the example Christ set for His followers: First
be a servant. Indeed, the idea of servant leadership
never fails to captivate. But while we study it, let us
remember its other hard lesson: no favorites.

A hard demand? Consider that it troubled even

Jesus. As He told His disciples, "Now that you know these things [about servant leadership], God will bless you for doing them" (John 13:17). *But not all of you.* "I know the ones I have chosen," He declared. For Jesus had handpicked Judas, too. But "the one who eats my food has turned against me" (v. 18).

And yet? He washed the feet of all twelve.

Even Judas.

So while we're busy being good servant leaders, will we serve even our enemies? Backstabbers? Betrayers? The ones plotting against and gossiping about us even right now?

The real servant leader doesn't have a choice. So stand up today and go wash feet. Yes, every one assigned to you. Then bless God by leaving what happens next in His hands, standing fast on His unmovable promise: "Now that you know these things, God will bless you for doing them." Believe it? Then go serve all.

The highest form of worship is the worship of unselfish Christian service.
BILLY GRAHAM

99

Service That Starts with Family

*"No," Peter protested. . . . Jesus replied,
"Unless I wash you, you won't belong to me."*

JOHN 13:8

Where to practice servanthood first? In the hardest place—right at home.

Jesus taught this lesson, not in the byways and highways of towns and villages, but in the bosom of His discipleship family. Right at the kitchen table.

He knew it's too easy to go across town and "serve" the poor when we haven't bothered to serve the people right at home.

Proud relatives would resist, for one thing.

So it embarrassed Peter, a beloved disciple, to receive from his Master the lowly work normally performed by a slave. Jesus even tied a slave's towel around His waist, laying aside His Lord clothes to pick up the foot-washing cloth of the lowliest servant.

Imagine your own most beloved relative— a grandparent or favorite aunt or uncle—kneeling on the ground before you to scrub off mud from your grimy, crusty feet.

But wait. That favorite grandparent did exactly that?

Or maybe it was a favorite teacher, camp counselor, or Sunday school teacher—that one golden person in your life who saw your need and gave all?

And now it's your turn. To suffer with a family member, performing the lowest tasks needed—like Jesus did.

Can you do it?

It will be hard. Unless you have a perfect family—and surely nobody does—it will be hard. Servanthood challenges ego and expertise. But Jesus set the standard. He gave all for people who weren't grateful. So let us, too, serve family, grateful or not. Then from that practice ground, let's go serve the world. God's reward, as He told Peter, will be His great and beautiful blessing.

The family fireside is the best of schools.
ARNOLD GLASOW

100

Completion That Gets the Job Done

It would be good for you to finish what you started.

2 Corinthians 8:10

I'm doing a brisk mile on the treadmill, eyes glued to a home renovation show called *Disaster DIY*. On this episode, the host is helping a retired mom "who started a thousand DIY [do it yourself] projects," says her daughter, "and she hasn't finished any of it." So the house is a disaster, for sure.

Kitchen floor? Loose tiles in place but never plastered down. Cabinets? Nailed in position, but the countertops wobble on top, unattached. Backsplash? Glass tiles are cut, but they're hanging on the wall with tape.

"Tape?" asks the show host, laughing with a wink.

But laughs turn to groans when he sees the bathroom, with its floor tiles "dry fit" but never installed and a bathtub with a plastic bag for a shower curtain. The biggest problem with this home owner?

"Confidence," says the host.

The home owner agrees. "And fear," she adds. Power tools and wet saws terrify her. So she stops short. Never completing anything.

The entire mess, however, makes me think about how, as believers, we struggle to finish this Christian walk with victory.

I reflect on the matter, in fact, as the HGTV host shows this homeowner how to chalk a plumb line across her kitchen floor before laying tile. Like our plumb line that is Christ, the chalk will mark the straight path to follow to achieve a tile floor that's right.

Can't find a friend to hold the other end of the line before snapping it? "Hang it on a nail." I listen to this advice, letting the words sink in. To be sure, if my life is attached to our Lord's crucifixion, I'll stay on track, walking this journey and finishing.

In that way, the homeowner "made a bit of a mess," as we do in life, "but she put her back into" the tasks and she finished. Beautiful kitchen? Even better, she earned a beautiful life. "I feel empowered," she said. Even better, in Christ, as we take on the tasks of life, we'll finish with beauty and grace.

The important thing is doing it.
BRYAN BAEUMLER

101

Completion That Honors the Sacrifice of Christ

*For by that one offering he forever made
perfect those who are being made holy.*

HEBREWS 10:14

Today I see a bright light. Not so big a light, but it's mighty. In a sea of bad news—that says only 68.8 percent of high school students in the United States graduate in four years—I discover the Urban Prep Academies, a public charter-school program in inner-city Chicago.

In three of the toughest neighborhoods in the nation, Urban Prep CEO Tim King and a determined faculty yearly see 100 percent of their graduates— including 107 boys in the all-black, all-male school's first graduating class—finish on top. So every Urban Prep graduate since 2010 has been accepted to a four-year college—Northwestern University, Morehouse College, Wheaton College, Howard University, and the University of Virginia, among others.

What fuels such achievement and completion?

Hard work and sacrifice, plus an extended school day that's two hours longer than most, and for good measure, students are assigned double periods of English.

Could we do as much in our living for Christ? To be sure, for 2010 graduate Krishaun Branch, who arrived at Urban Prep with Ds and truancies, the road to becoming president of the school's student government association was all sacrifice.

"I knew I was going down the wrong path," he told the Associated Press. "I had to graduate or my life was going to be nothing."

The result of his sacrifice? "My personality changed. My posture changed. My speech changed. A lot about me has changed."

Sound familiar? As followers of Christ, when we sacrifice our all to reach a goal, we, too, will discover a fresh walk, graduating from old ways to new change. As new creatures in the Lord, we even look different. Our great inspiration, indeed, is Christ. Let us bless Him today by pursuing a goal that honors His selfless, finalizing sacrifice. Then let's finish it.

He finished it when He couldn't, but He did.
LESTER ROLOFF

Endnotes

DAY

2 *"I wait quietly"* Richard Foster, *Prayer: Finding the Heart's True Home* (New York: HarperCollins, 1992), 200.

12 *"This is just unbelievable"* "4 Weeks after Quake, Survivor Found," WPLG–Miami, February 9, 2010.

15 *"As we start on the miracle"* Lewis Smedes, *The Art of Forgiving: When You Need to Forgive and Don't Know How* (New York: Ballantine Books, 1996), 6.

16 *"is to refuse"* Charles Spurgeon, *Morning and Evening*, trans. Alistair Begg, (Wheaton, IL: Crossway Books, 2003), 609.

16 *"the spiritual razzmatazz"* John Reed, "Luke," J. Reed's Christian Expositions, http://www.jrtalks.com/Luke /luke17v11to19.html.

18 *"My prayer [hopes]"* Andrew Murray, *With Christ in the School of Prayer* (New Kensington, PA: Whitaker House, 1981), 165.

20 *"The principle of tithing"* Crown Financial Ministries, "What Ministers Should Teach," http://www.crown.org/Articles /tabid/107/entryid/84/Default.aspx.

30 *In the book* Making Room Christine D. Pohl, *Making Room: Recovering Hospitality as a Christian Tradition* (Grand Rapids, MI: Eerdmans, 1999).

42 *"constitutional sins"* Arthur Pink, "Self Knowledge," *Studies in the Scriptures* 7 1934–35, 46.

45 *"don't ask Him to forgive"* R. C. Sproul, *The Intimate Marriage* (Phillipsburg, NJ: P&R Publishing, 1975), 127–128.

46 *"The quality of mercy"* William Shakespeare, *The Merchant of Venice*, act 4, scene 1.

52 *"the everlasting burden"* Richard Foster, *Celebration of Discipline: The Path to Spiritual Growth*, 3rd ed. (San Francisco: HarperSanFrancisco, 1988), 10.

53 *"the most popular living person"* Catharine Smith, "Facebook's Most Popular: The 50 Hottest People on Facebook," *Huffington Post*, July 9, 2010, http://www.huffingtonpost .com/2010/07/09/facebook-most-popular-the_n_640965 .html#s111758&title=1__Michael.

53 *"Celebrities are fascinating"* Carlin Flora, "Seeing by Starlight: Celebrity Obsession," *Psychology Today*, http://www.psychologytoday.com/ articles/200407/seeing-starlight-celebrity-obsession.

55 *"Retire from the world"* A. W. Tozer, "Of God and Men: Cultivating the Divine/Human Relationship," *Christian Publications*, June 1995, 128–129.

57 *Yet daily prayer, unlike five other faith habits* Barna Group, "Five Out of Seven Core Religious Behaviors Have Increased in the Past Decade According to Barna Survey," April 3, 2006, http://www.barna.org/barna-update/article /5-barna-update/156-five-out-of-seven-core-religious -behaviors-have-increased-in-the-past-decade-according-to -barna-survey?q=prayer.

61 *"We rested in God's love"* Lynne M. Baab, "The Gift of Rest," *Today's Christian Woman*, September/October 2005, 36, http://www.todayschristianwoman.com/articles/2005 /september/7.36.html.

64 *"I believe that there are hundreds"* Associated Press, "DNA Exonerates Dallas County Man after 26 Years in Prison,"

Houston Chronicle, January 3, 2008, http://www.chron.com
/disp/story.mpl/headline/metro/5422726.html.

64 *In fact, if just one percent* See *The Innocence Project Annual
Report 2010*, http://www.innocenceproject.org/files
/imported/2010innocenceprojectannualreport.pdf.

68 *As delightful as an eleven-year-old* You can read about these
stories at http://www.msnbc.msn.com/id/34455093/ns
/us_news-wonderful_world/ and http://www.msnbc.msn
.com/id/40630483/ns/us_news-wonderful_world/.

75 *"for survival, not for navigation" NLT Study Bible* (Carol
Stream, IL: Tyndale House Publishers, 2008), 33.

80 *"It is exactly this balance"* "Enjoying God's Gifts" in *NLT
Study Bible* (Carol Stream, IL: Tyndale House Publishers,
2008), 1077.

86 *"These findings"* Ted Baehr, *So You Want to Be in Pictures*
(Nashville: Broadman and Holman Publishers, 2005), 67.

88 *"Learning self-discipline"* John MacArthur, *The Pillars of
Christian Character: The Essential Attitudes of a Living Faith*
(Wheaton, IL: Crossway Books, 1998), 139.

93 *Americans have the highest levels* Jennifer Warner, "U.S.
Leads the World in Illegal Drug Use," CBS News.com,
July 1, 2008, http://www.cbsnews.com/stories/2008/07/01
/health/webmd/main4222322.shtml.

95 *"From start to finish"* E. M. Bounds, *The Necessity of Prayer*
(Radford, VA: Wilder Publications, 2008), 61.

97 *"It lacked the power" NLT Study Bible* (Carol Stream, IL:
Tyndale House Publishers, 2008), 1263.

100 *a retired mom* "*who started a thousand*" "Tiling Crackdown:
Episode HDDIY-402H," *Disaster DIY*, HGTV.

101 *"I knew I was going"* Sharon Cohen, "100 Percent of Urban
Prep's First Class College-Bound," Associated Press, June 28,
2010.

About the Author

Award-winning author of Tyndale's *I Told the Mountain to Move* (a Book of the Year finalist in *Christianity Today*'s 2006 Book Awards competition), Patricia is also author of the critically acclaimed *My First White Friend*, which won a Christopher Award, and *The One Year God's Great Blessings Devotional*. With her daughter Alana, she coauthored the memoir *Undivided: A Muslim Daughter, Her Christian Mother, Their Path to Peace*. Her personal essays have been published in the *New York Times Magazine*, *Newsweek*, *USA Today*, *USA Weekend*, the *Chicago Tribune*, In Touch Ministries' *In Touch* magazine, *Christianity Today*, and several blogs including *The High Calling* and *Her.meneutics*. Her essays have also aired on National Public Radio. Formerly a Sunday magazine editor at the *Denver Post* and a features reporter at the *Rocky Mountain News* in Denver, she taught print journalism at the University of Colorado at Boulder for fifteen years and now writes full-time on matters of faith. She's a regular contributor to the *Today's Christian Woman* blog and serves on the board of the Colorado Authors' League. A lifetime Colorado resident, Patricia and her husband, Dan, have two grown daughters and five grandchildren. She tackles topics that challenge believers to bridge their divides by drawing closer to one another with Christ. Join her on the journey at www.patriciaraybon.com.

GOD'S GREAT BLESSINGS
DEVOTIONAL *a daily guide*
by PATRICIA RAYBON

Want God's breakthrough
blessings in your life? Every
day? Get on the pathway to
God's best for you through
*The One Year God's Great
Blessings Devotional.*
Discover the enriching
secrets of a bold Christian
life as you learn fifty-two
biblical virtues that bless
God, bless His world—
and, in return, greatly
bless you!

ISBN 978-1-4143-3871-2

SIMPLE MOMENTS THAT WILL REVIVE YOUR SPIRIT AND RENEW YOUR HEART

978-1-4964-1162-4

Sometimes we're running so fast it's hard to find time for the things that matter most. Kim Newlen shares encouraging insights in *Sweet and Simple Moments with God*, inspiring us to take a sweet and simple moment to be still with God every day. Make every moment count through spending time with the One who can carry your burdens best.

CP1066